Native Americans

VOLUME 9

SCALPING–TOBACCO

GROLIER

About this book

Thousands of years ago groups of hunter-gatherers from Asia began crossing the Bering Strait land bridge, which temporarily linked Siberia and Alaska. These earliest American settlers found a land of extreme environmental contrasts. Over the centuries the groups—ancestors of Native Americans—settled throughout North and South America, forming tribes and creating cultures and lifestyles that were influenced by their local environment. As in all parts of the world, conflicts emerged between the different tribes, but it was not until the arrival of Europeans in the late 15th and early 16th centuries that the survival of all Native Americans began to be threatened. Warfare, disease, and first European then American expansion combined to rid Native Americans of their homeland and, in most cases, their way of life. In the process whole tribes were wiped out, but many have survived. And for those that have, modern life has brought new challenges, cultural and political, that nonnative Americans are beginning to be made aware of.

There are 10 volumes in this set profiling all of the major Native-American groups, the history of their lives in each region, and background anthropology, archaeology, and other topics key to understanding Native Americans. Each volume contains entries ranging from important Native-American events and figures to wide-ranging beliefs and customs, an A–Z of some 90 tribes, and an index that covers the whole set. Also, each entry is fully illustrated with pictures, photographs, or maps and concludes with a list of cross-references to other entries in the set. This means readers can refer to each volume as a series of stories or cross-reference from one volume to another, following a subject that particularly interests them.

Published 2000 by Grolier Educational
Sherman Turnpike
Danbury, Connecticut 06816

Reprinted in 2001

© 2000 Brown Partworks Ltd

Set ISBN: 0-7172-9395-5
Volume ISBN: 0-7172-9404-8

Cover picture: Peter Newark Historical Pictures

For information address the publisher:
Grolier Educational, Sherman Turnpike,
Danbury, Connecticut 06816

Library of Congress Cataloging-in-Publication Data
Native Americans
p.cm.—Includes index.—Contents: v.1. Acoma–basketry—v.2. Bat cave–children—v.3. Chinook–education—v.4. El Tajín–Huron—v.5. Indian claims commission–longhouse religion—v.6. Mangas Coloradas–Muskogean speakers—v.7. Naskapi–Pontiac's war—v.8. Population density–Sauk and Fox—v.9. Scalping–tobacco—v.10. Toltec–Zuni.
1. Indians of North America Encyclopedia. Juvenile. [1. Indians of North America Encyclopedia.]
E76.2.N375 1999   99-28319
970.004'97'003—dc21   CIP

For Brown Partworks Ltd
CONSULTANT: Norman Bancroft Hunt
MANAGING EDITOR: Dawn Titmus
PROJECT EDITOR: Lee Stacy
ART DIRECTOR: Bradley Davis
DESIGNER: Paul Griffin
TEXT EDITORS: Robert Dimery, Peter Harrison,
    Lol Henderson, and Patrick Newman
PICTURE RESEARCH: Susannah Jayes and Rebecca Watson
INDEX: Kay Ollerenshaw
MAPS: William Lebihan

Printed in Singapore

CONTENTS

Scalping

Scalping is the removal of hair and skin from the head of an enemy. It was widely practiced in North America, especially among tribes of the Great Plains.

Early European observers reported scalping as a barbaric Native-American custom, but its true origin is obscure. Some historians believe scalping was introduced by Europeans, while others think it developed independently in North America. Current opinion is that scalping was known to Native Americans before they encountered Europeans, but that Europeans began paying for scalps, which made scalping a major source of income for many settlers as well.

HONOR OR BOUNTY

Native Americans believed scalping was an honor paid to a defeated warrior who had fought bravely. By taking the scalp, they thought they captured the victim's soul, or spirit, which was said to reside in the hair. Native Americans believed the soul of the victim would then accompany the victor's soul in the underworld— a great honor.

Although they shared this belief in capturing the enemy's soul, attitudes among tribes varied widely. Most scalps were a small piece of hair taken from the crown of the head, inflicting a painful but not necessarily fatal wound. However, some Siouan tribes took the entire head-hair and also parts of the face. In contrast, the Pima and Papago of the Southwest took only four hairs as a symbolic scalp and followed this with a 14-day purification rite. The Apache took no scalps at all.

ABOVE: Scalps were regarded as war trophies by Plains tribes.

Europeans, however, considered scalps as proof of a killing and paid bounties to anyone who brought back enemy scalps. Bounty hunters were encouraged to wipe out local tribes and free their lands for settlement. Men, women, and children were killed in the interests of European expansion, and their scalps were displayed to the public. Even during the 19th century the states of Sonora and Chihuahua in Mexico were paying bounties for the scalps of dead Apache.

SEE ALSO:
❖ Afterlife
❖ Apache
❖ Plains
❖ Sand Creek Massacre
❖ Warriors

Scouts

The tracking skills of Native Americans were legendary and were made use of by hunters, explorers, trappers, and various military units from the start of the European presence in North America.

In the 19th century many U.S. Army units were able to locate the camps of their enemies only by using Native-American scouts. General Crook, in 1871, used Apache scouts from the reservations to find the mountain strongholds of hostile Apache groups. Major Frank North organized a division of Pawnee scouts during the 1860s and 1870s to protect railroad crews. Custer was warned by Crow scouts of the strength of the Sioux and Cheyenne camps at Little Bighorn but disastrously chose to ignore their advice.

UNCANNY ABILITIES

Soldiers who saw Native-American scouts in action were amazed at how well they could track. Scouts could follow a trail over hard ground on which soldiers could see no marks at all. They were often able to say which tribe the tracks were made by, how many people were in the group, the direction they were moving in, and how long it had been since they had passed by.

Most scouts signed on for a limited period of service, usually six months. Many saw scouting as an opportunity to escape from the routine of reservation life. Most wore blue U.S. Army jackets and red headbands so soldiers could tell they were friendly. They were led by chief scouts, who were usually whites they respected.

ABOVE: Corporal "Rattlesnake," shown here, was a Pawnee scout who served under Major Frank North in the 1860s and 1870s.

Although Native-American scouts served the United States loyally, the government paid little regard to this. At the end of hostilities most of the scouts were imprisoned along with the hostile Native Americans they had helped track down.

SEE ALSO:
- Apache
- Cheyenne
- Cochise
- Crow
- Geronimo
- Interpreters
- Little Bighorn
- Pawnee
- Railroads
- Reservations
- Sacajawea
- Sioux

Seattle, Chief

Seattle, who was also called Seathl or Sealth, was born about 1790. His mother was Duwamish; his father, Squamish. He became chief of both these tribes, as well as chief of several other Salish-speaking tribes in the Puget Sound area of the Northwest Coast.

At the time of Seattle's birth the Spanish, British, and Russians were exploring the Northwest Coast, but no Europeans had settled in the region. Then in the early 19th century the area began to attract fur traders and settlers to its virgin forests and lush farmland.

CONVERSION TO CHRISTIANITY

In the 1830s missionaries began to arrive on the Northwest Coast. Catholic missionaries from Quebec converted Seattle, who was previously a fearless warrior. He then started morning and evening church services among his people and argued for peace with settlers. Impressed by his friendliness, the settlers in Puget Sound named their settlement after him in 1852.

Seattle objected to this at first because according to his tribal beliefs, his spirit would be disturbed each time his name was mentioned. But in his final years he agreed to allow the city now called Seattle to use his name in return for a small tax paid to his family to compensate for the disturbance to his spirit.

In 1855 Seattle signed the Port Elliott Treaty, giving up his people's lands on Puget Sound for new lands on seven reservations. He agreed himself to move to the Port Madison reservation. But not all the Salish welcomed the large numbers

ABOVE: This portrait depicts Seattle in his later years. He spent his last 10 years on the reservation at Port Madison, dying there on June 7, 1866, aged over 70.

of settlers, and in the fall of 1855 many of them launched a campaign of resistance that lasted for several years. Seattle, however, stood by the treaty until the end of his life.

SEE ALSO:
- Fur Trade
- Missions
- Northwest Coast
- Reservations
- Salish
- Settlers
- Treaties

Seminole

The Seminole are a group of Native Americans who migrated during the early 1700s from Georgia to Florida, which at the time was owned by the Spanish.

The Seminole were mostly from the Creek tribe, but they were also joined by other tribes, such as the Yuchi, Yamasee, and Choctaw. Many of these tribespeople were escaping slavery in the British-controlled northern colonies. They settled in and around the Everglades area, bravely defending their way of life and their independence over a period of almost 200 years.

The name "Seminole" comes from the Creek word "Simanóle," meaning "separatist" or "runaway," and describes a people who made their home in the swamps, where they were joined by many Native-American war refugees and runaway African slaves. The Seminole hid the black slaves and welcomed them into their families. Over the years these Africans married into the tribe and became known as "Black Seminole."

SEMINOLE LIFESTYLE

The Seminole were fishers and hunters, hunting deer, wild turkey, alligator, turtle, and other game. They also gathered fruit, nuts, and berries. Once the tribe settled, they became farmers, growing corn, sugarcane, guava, and bananas. They also raised cattle and horses. Seminole children were encouraged to help with the chores, such as gathering wood for fires.

The houses the Seminole built in the Florida swamps were ideally suited to the warm, wet conditions

there. They had pole foundations, open sides, thatched roofs, and small attics for storage. These houses, called "chickees," were high enough out of the water to stay dry, while the open sides let in cool air. Each house accommodated one family, though there were also communal cooking houses.

ABOVE: Charles Bird King painted this portrait of Chief Tukosee Mathla, a Seminole chief, in 1826.

For transport the Seminole made dugout canoes with a platform at the back. A person could stand on this platform and push the boat with a long pole that reached to the bottom of the swamp.

WAR WITH THE U.S.

In 1812 the Seminole learned that a group of slaveowners from Georgia was planning to raid their settlements. To preempt this raid, they attacked the Georgians on their own plantations. The U.S. government then sent troops into Florida, led by General Andrew Jackson, who became known to Native

BELOW: These Seminole dancers are wearing the traditional dress of their tribe. They are performing the Round Dance, which was held for a variety of festivals throughout the year.

Americans as "sharp knife." General Jackson's troops looted and burned Native-American villages. In 1816 forces under General Edmund Gaines attacked a settlement of Black Seminole and killed most of the inhabitants, taking the survivors back as slaves. The following year the First Seminole War began when General Jackson once again crossed the border and destroyed more Seminole villages.

The U.S. bought Florida from the Spanish in 1819. Settlers soon began to move into the area and to drive out the Native Americans. On May 28, 1830, the Indian Removal Act

Fact File

LANGUAGE:	*Muskogean*
AREA:	*Florida*
RESERVATION:	*Southern Florida and Oklahoma*
POPULATION:	*100,000 Pre-Contact; approximately 13,800 today*
HOUSING:	*Chickees, swamp pole-and-thatch houses*
EUROPEAN CONTACT:	*Spanish conquistadors in 16th century; European settlers in 18th century*
NEIGHBORS:	*Creek, Choctaw, and Chickasaw*
LIFESTYLE:	*Fishing, hunting, and gathering*
FOOD:	*Fish, shellfish, corn, wild fruit, and small game*
CRAFTS:	*Patchwork and appliqué clothing*

The Seminole lived in the Everglades and maintained their independence for almost 200 years.

was passed, forcing many Native Americans onto reservations in the Indian Territory (present-day Oklahoma). The act was pushed through by Andrew Jackson, who was by then president of the United States.

The first tribes to be moved to the Indian Territory were the so-called Five Civilized Tribes—the Seminole, Choctaw, Creek, Chickasaw, and Cherokee.

The tribes were called "civilized" because, like Europeans and Americans, they lived in villages and farmed. Some of them also became Christians and adopted nonnative styles of dress. The Seminole in particular had a characteristic way of dressing, part-European and part-Native American, with clothes made from brightly colored patchwork.

TRAIL OF TEARS
The removal of the Five Tribes became known as the "Trail of Tears." Thousands of Native Americans were forced by troops to march to the land reserved for them in the Indian Territory. Many men, women,

and children died of hunger, cold, and disease on the long journey. Survivors were not even allowed to stop and bury their dead. But the Seminole fiercely resisted being forced off their lands, and this resistance led to the Second Seminole War.

THE SECOND SEMINOLE WAR
The leader of the Seminole at this time was Chief Osceola. He was not a hereditary chief but had risen to lead his people because of his brave stand against white settlers. With a small band of warriors he defeated U.S. troops at the Battle of Withlacoochee in Citrus County. The army then lured Osceola and his advisors to a peace meeting and captured them.

Osceola died in prison, but two of his men, Wild Cat and John Horse, escaped. The army troops who pursued them were ambushed and defeated by Seminole tribespeople. Further battles ensued, and the war dragged on until 1842, costing the U.S. government many lives and over 20 million dollars.

LEFT: This photograph shows Seminole dolls in traditional dress.

THE THIRD SEMINOLE WAR

In 1855 the Third Seminole War broke out when Seminole chief Billy Bowlegs attacked the U.S. military in Collier County. This time the war lasted for three years. At the end of this period most of the Seminole had been forced onto the Indian Territory, and only a few remained in the Everglades. On the Indian Territory the Seminole came into conflict with the Creek. There was not enough land or food for both tribes, and resentments grew.

The situation was made worse in 1887 when the Allotment Act was passed. The act declared that only individuals, not tribes, could own land and that settlers could buy any remaining land. These rules created conflict among the tribes, and much of the land eventually ended up in the hands of settlers.

In 1934 the Indian Reorganization Act was passed to try to improve life for Native-American tribes. Under the act many tribes formed their own councils with their own constitutions and were given government aid for the provision of health care, education, and cultural projects.

In 1957 the Seminole Tribe of Florida was formally created. However, those tribespeople who spoke the Mikosuki language split away from this tribe to form the Miccosukee Tribe of Florida. Today both groups have reservations in Florida and in Oklahoma.

Seminole Wars

During the War of 1812 the Seminole sided with the British against the Americans. At the time the tribe further angered the U.S. government by harboring escaped African-American slaves (called "Freedmen"). Since Florida was then a Spanish colony, and Spanish–Seminole relations were very good, it was difficult for slaveowners to recapture their "property."

HOSTILITIES BREAK OUT

Armed clashes with the Seminole in 1816 and 1817 led the U.S. to plan a full-scale attack against the tribe. An invasion of Florida began in March 1818 under General Andrew Jackson.

Jackson's troops destroyed many Seminole villages and captured the Spanish capital at Pensacola in May. Spain had few resources to oppose this attack and began talks with the U.S. government. The resulting Adams–Onís Treaty of 1819 made Florida part of the U.S. and therefore a region where slave-owning was legal. After Jackson's attacks most Seminole and Red Stick Creek were forced to move to the swampy lake-land areas of northern Florida and near modern Orlando and Tampa.

THE FIGHT AGAINST REMOVAL

White settlers flooded in to Florida through the 1820s, and as a result many Creek were forced to move from Florida to the Indian Territory (now Oklahoma). In the early 1830s the remaining Seminole came under increasing pressure to move also.

A few Seminole leaders reluctantly signed the Treaty of Paynes Landing (1832), which stated that the tribe should move to the Indian Territory within three years. The treaty was soon rejected by the tribe as a whole, but the U.S. began reinforcing its troops in Florida to force the Seminole to comply.

BELOW: This painting depicts the ambush of a U.S. Army supply wagon by Seminole warriors near St. Augustine, Florida, in 1812. At the time the Seminole were allied with the British.

LEFT: In this painting a group of Seminole are shown attacking a fort blockhouse. A blockhouse was a small fortified building that could be easily defended against attackers. This incident occurred on December 25, 1837, during the second of the three Seminole Wars.

MORE WARS WITH THE U.S.

A chief called Osceola now emerged as the main Seminole leader. Faced with the threat of removal, Osceola began a rebellion in November 1835 by killing another Seminole leader who had agreed to move to the Indian Territory. This signaled the start of the Second Seminole War.

Osceola and other chiefs launched a series of raids on U.S. Army forts and white settlements. They won a major victory in late December when over 100 U.S. soldiers were killed in one attack during the so-called Dade Massacre. During the years of bitter fighting that followed, the Seminole made good use of their knowledge of how to survive in the swamplands. Using guerrilla tactics, they repeatedly outwitted American troops who tried to hunt them down.

Osceola was an exceptional military leader, but in October 1837 he was captured after attending fake peace talks. He died in jail in South Carolina in early 1838. In December 1837 U.S. forces under General Zachary Taylor won a major battle, at Lake Okeechobee, during which many Seminole were killed.

REMOVAL AND PEACE AT LAST

Over the next few years several thousand Seminole moved to the Indian Territory, but armed clashes continued until 1842. In that year the U.S. gave up trying to prise the Seminole from their last strongholds deep in the Everglades. From 1855 to 1858 the tribe fought the Third Seminole War to try to stop further white incursions into their territory.

After this final confrontation, only about 200 Seminole opted to remain in Florida. Many Seminole moved to the Indian Territory. Their descendants did not make a formal peace with the U.S. until 1962, when their ownership of the lands where they still live—Seminole County in Oklahoma—was confirmed.

SEE ALSO:
❖ Five Civilized Tribes
❖ Indian Territory
❖ Osceola
❖ Seminole
❖ Settlers
❖ Southeast/ Florida
❖ Spain, Wars with

Sequoyah

Sequoyah, a Cherokee, was perhaps the only individual to develop an alphabet from scratch. He was a warrior, hunter, trader, and silversmith, but it is for his language skills that he is remembered. His writing system turned Cherokee from a purely spoken form into a written language within a few short years.

Sequoyah started work on his alphabet in 1809. After trying pictographs (small pictures used to represent words), he developed a phonetic system—a set of symbols that represents the 85 sounds made in the Cherokee language.

His system was completed in 1821, and the Cherokee rapidly adopted it—some claim that they were a literate nation by 1822. The written word had a big impact on the tribe, and by 1828 the first Cherokee-language newspaper, *The Cherokee Phoenix*, was set up. The Cherokee themselves referred to the newspaper as "talking leaves."

THE POWER OF WRITING

Sequoyah recognized that the power of written language gave Europeans and white Americans a big advantage over the Cherokee. Writing enabled information to be transmitted and used much more efficiently than was possible with oral tradition and fallible memory. Sequoyah felt that if the Cherokee were to survive, they needed to adopt writing.

By the early 19th century some Cherokee were already using written English. Sequoyah himself knew English, Spanish, and French by the time he was a young man, and *The Cherokee Phoenix* was also published in the English language.

RIGHT: Sequoyah developed an alphabet for the Cherokee nation in 1821. This painting of him is by C. B. Wilson.

SEE ALSO:
- Education
- Five Civilized Tribes
- Indian Territory
- Literature
- Trail of Tears

Just as he opposed U.S. encroachment on Cherokee lands, Sequoyah was determined to resist the destruction of his people's culture. He wanted Cherokee to be a written language in its own right. Sequoyah died aged 83 in 1843, knowing that because of his work the Cherokee language would endure.

Serpent Mound

Serpent Mound is situated on a limestone plateau above the valley of Brush Creek in Adams County, Ohio. It is an earth mound representing the body of a snake and uncoils for almost a quarter of a mile (0.4 km) over the surrounding area.

Serpent Mound is one of the few examples of an effigy mound (a mound built in the shape of an animal, bird, or human) in Ohio. It is also the finest and largest snake effigy in the U.S. and possibly the world. Today Serpent Mound is the centerpiece of the state memorial park surrounding it.

THE STRANGE SERPENT

The effigy is made up of a series of mounds that resembles a moving snake with seven "waves" or curves in its body and three coils in its tail. The mounds range from 4 to 6 feet (1.2 to 1.8 m) in height and between 4 to 20 feet (1.2 to 6 m) in width.

The snake's mouth is open and encloses a huge oval. Some scholars believe the oval is an egg that the snake is swallowing. Others suggest it is a frog or the snake's own heart. It has also been suggested that the oval is the serpent's open mouth seen head-on. Since the snake extends westward, the oval may also represent the setting sun. The total length of the snake, including this oval, is 1,400 feet (424 m).

Unlike many prehistoric earthworks, the Serpent Mound runs down from the crescent of a gently sloping hill. This means the effigy can be seen from the valley floor.

THE MOUND MAKERS

It is not known who the builders of Serpent Mound were. Effigy mounds were not used for burials, so they contain no artifacts associated with burial customs that may have helped identify their makers.

Suggestions for the identity of the mound builders have ranged from European travelers to Native Americans from Central America. However, archaeological investigations of the site have failed to find any artifacts that may have provided clues to the builders or the meaning of the effigy.

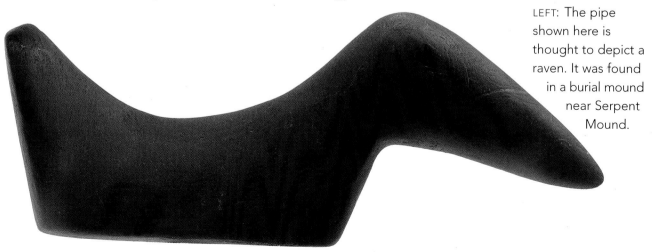

ABOVE: The Adena and Hopewell used stone pestles such as this one found near Serpent Mound to grind corn.

LEFT: The pipe shown here is thought to depict a raven. It was found in a burial mound near Serpent Mound.

Nearby, however, archaeologists have excavated a series of cone-shaped mounds that have provided clues to the possible identity of the mound makers. Artifacts, including stone ax-heads, arrowheads, and a copper breastplate, characteristic of the Adena Native Americans, have been found. The Adena lived in the Ohio Valley between 1000 B.C. and A.D. 200. Some experts suspect they were responsible for the earthworks.

THE MYSTERIOUS MOUND
The precise meaning of Serpent Mound remains a mystery. Snakes have symbolized both good and evil in many religions, and their significance to the makers of the mound is still uncertain. However, the careful planning and the enormous labor involved in carrying thousands of baskets of earth to the site clearly reflect the importance of the earthwork to its builders.

Today some Native Americans regard Serpent Mound as a sacred site. Many have campaigned to save the site from any plans to flood the surrounding valley for commercial development. Whatever its original purpose, Serpent Mound stands today as a tribute to the ingenuity of ancient Native-American builders.

ABOVE: In this photograph of Serpent Mound the serpent's head is to the right, and its tail is to the left.

SEE ALSO:
❖ Adena and Hopewell
❖ Mississippian
❖ Mound City
❖ Mound Spiro
❖ Sacred Sites

Settlers

The relationship between Native Americans and settlers was a complex one, and there were many misunderstandings on both sides. In general Native Americans could not understand the settlers' wish to own the lands they lived on. For their part the settlers could not understand the Native-American belief that land was sacred and could not be the property of any one individual.

The early settlers came primarily from four different European nations—Spain, France, England, and the Netherlands. Groups from each country had their own reasons for wishing to settle in North America. Each adopted a different policy toward the Native Americans whom they encountered.

Each of the European nations that sent settlers to North America was driven by a strong desire for exploration. They were aided in this by advances in marine technology, such as better navigational aids. In 1492 the explorer Christopher Columbus had suggested the New World had a wealth of economic resources for Europeans to exploit. Many settlers also wished to escape from religious conflicts between Protestants and Catholics in their own countries. The Americas seemed to offer opportunities for a new start.

COLONIZING NORTH AMERICA

The first European settlement in North America was St. Augustine in Florida, which the Spanish built in 1565. The Spanish also explored the Southwest and established Santa Fe in New Mexico in 1609.

Meanwhile, England was forming its own colonies. Jamestown in Virginia was founded in 1607, and

BELOW: In this hand-colored woodcut the Pilgrim Fathers are depicted building their settlement at Plymouth in Cape Cod Bay.

the Pilgrims arrived in Massachusetts in 1620. Dutch and French interests were centered on the economic benefits of the fur trade rather than on permanent settlements. However, they both also formed fairly large communities in New York (Dutch—originally "New Amsterdam") and Canada (French).

Most of the early settlers cooperated with the Native Americans they came into contact with. Indeed, Jamestown survived its early years only because the colonists there received some support from a confederacy of tribes called the Powhatan. French interests were also served by friendly contacts. These included marriages between French and Native Americans that led to the formation of a mixed-blood group, the Métis, in Canada.

These early friendships quickly deteriorated when Europeans, particularly the English, demanded Native-American lands for their plantations. The colony of Virginia, which had come to rely on tobacco-growing after Sir Walter Raleigh brought tobacco to Europe, wanted room for growing the crop. Conflicts arose both between the settlers and Native Americans and between the different European powers.

AN ATTEMPT AT COMPROMISE

To avoid conflict and keep the Native Americans and the settlers apart, Great Britain declared the Proclamation Line in 1763. It was intended to make land west of the Mississippi an area for Native Americans where white settlement was forbidden, leaving the eastern regions for Europeans. However,

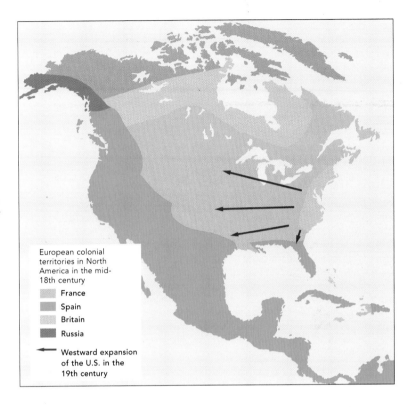

European colonial territories in North America in the mid-18th century

░░ France

▨ Spain

▒ Britain

▓ Russia

← Westward expansion of the U.S. in the 19th century

ABOVE: Beginning in the early 16th century, European settlers began colonizing North America and in the process displacing whole tribes. The spread of white settlers continued until the end of the 19th century. This map illustrates the European territorial claims to North America until the mid-18th century and later the expansion of U.S. settlers across the continent.

the Proclamation Line lasted only a short time and was ignored after the American Revolution of 1776. Settlers often illegally established themselves in the country the Native Americans thought had been reserved exclusively for their use.

The newly formed United States government tried to resolve these issues by making treaties with the different tribes. These treaties meant tribes gave up many of their rights and allowed settlement outside areas previously occupied by colonists. Some treaties were clearly fraudulent. Bribery, the use of "treaty chiefs" who had no authority, and the deliberate misinterpretation of agreements led many tribes to sign away their lands in return for benefits they never received.

The United States government also realized there would be conflict between Native Americans living in

the treaty areas and white settlers who wished to claim these lands. The Indian Removal Act of the 1830s enabled the U.S. to forcibly remove tribes from their original homelands if these were wanted for settlement. Many of the disputes between Native Americans and the U.S. that continue to this day stem from this ill-considered policy of treating Native Americans as people without rights to territories they originally occupied.

DIVIDING UP THE LAND

Matters came to a head in 1862 with the Homestead Act, which opened up Native-American lands in Kansas and Nebraska to white settlement. The Allotment Act of 1887 was an attempt to break up the reservations. It gave each Native-American family 160 acres (65 ha) of land but took away any tribal control. However, this was too small an area for Native

Americans who depended on hunting for survival. Many families sold or leased their land to settlers so they could receive some income to support themselves.

The colonizing of North America paid little attention to Native-American needs. Many settlements grew into major cities in Canada and the United States. To allow for this expansion, Native Americans were increasingly pushed into areas that are only a fraction of the land they originally occupied.

ABOVE: This painting by Oscar Berninghaus depicts Native Americans watching the relentless flow of wagon trains across their lands in the West.

SEE ALSO:
- ❖ Allotment Act
- ❖ Columbus, Christopher
- ❖ Disenfranchisement
- ❖ Fur Trade
- ❖ Land Rights
- ❖ Manifest Destiny
- ❖ Métis
- ❖ Powhatan, Chief
- ❖ Powhatan Wars
- ❖ Southwest
- ❖ Treaties
- ❖ Wagon Trails

Shamanism

Scholars use the term "shamanism" to describe a type of religious practice followed by many Native-American peoples. The word "shaman" is not Native-American. It comes from the Tungus people of Siberia and means "wise one." European colonists and explorers who saw shamans curing the sick often described them as "medicine men" or "medicine women" instead. However, shamans' skill as healers

RIGHT: In this illustration from the 19th century a shaman (medicine man) uses his special powers to treat a patient.

ABOVE: This photograph of a Native-American Blood Indian shaman wearing a ritual headdress was taken in 1880.

THE SUPERNATURAL WORLD

The shamans were thought to be capable of doing so many different things because of the influence they had with the spirits of the supernatural world. In Native-American belief everything has a spirit, or soul. This spirit can be persuaded to use its power for the people's benefit when asked to do so by a shaman acting on behalf of the community.

Only certain people were able to become shamans. They were usually highly gifted and perceptive individuals. However, gaining shamanic ability was a long and difficult process that demanded stamina and courage. This was because the spirit allies, or guides, of the shamans "tested" them in many ways. These tests could take the form of sickness for the shaman or his or her family, terrible nightmares, misfortune, or other ordeals. Only by passing these tests could the shaman gain experience and progress to higher levels of spiritual awareness and a deeper understanding of the ways of the supernatural world.

was only one of the abilities they possessed. They were thought to be capable of discovering lost property and of bringing game animals close to the camps so that hunting would be easier. Native-American shamans were also thought to have the power to control the weather.

Because of their skills in curing and in controlling matters that were essential to the people's survival, the shamans were often very powerful members of their communities. The famous leader of the Hunkpapa Sioux, Sitting Bull, was actually a shaman rather than a chief.

SHAMAN GUIDES

Most shamans—even experienced ones—usually had a guide or helper to assist them through the most difficult parts of their lives. This guide was often an older shaman or sometimes even a spirit being.

The guide passed on techniques of surviving the more serious hazards of a shamanic life and taught the shaman how to make and keep good relations with the spirit world. A shaman often made contact with spirits after undergoing long periods of fasting, thirsting, and loss of sleep. These experiences were physically and psychologically demanding. When they were over, the shaman entered a comalike state, or trance, in which he or she experienced dreams, or visions, in which spirits gave advice or warnings.

SHAMANISM AND CHRISTIANITY

Shamans had powerful positions in their societies and were very much in harmony with the spiritual world of Native Americans. For these reasons European priests and missionaries often considered the shamans to be the main opposition to the conversion of tribes to Christianity.

To the priests and missionaries the legends the shamans retold and the visions they experienced were superstitious beliefs that had to be stamped out and replaced by Christian ideas. They sometimes claimed the shamans were wizards and witches who were helped by the Devil, though the idea of a "devil" was European and not something that Native Americans believed in.

The shamans have been persecuted for their religious beliefs since the time of early European contact in the

RIGHT: This raven rattle is used in healing rituals by Northwest Coast shamans.

15th century. This continued under U.S. domination in the 19th and early 20th centuries. It was not until the Indian Religion Freedom Act of 1934 that practicing shamanism without fear of persecution was recognized as a legal right of Native Americans living in the U.S.

A SPIRITUAL ALTERNATIVE

Since the 1960s and 1970s shamanism has become popular with many nonnative people. This new group of followers sees it as an escape from the material demands of modern society and as a way of leading a more spiritual life. Many of these new shamanic movements use ideas and techniques that originated with Native Americans.

On a different level Native-American shamans have begun working very successfully with professional hospital staff such as doctors, surgeons, and psychologists, treating both Native-American and nonnative patients.

In modern tribal communities shamans are once again regarded as important. They are helping rebuild a sense of history and dignity in traditional religious beliefs. By retelling ancient legends and acting out tribal rituals, shamans are insuring that future generations of Native Americans will not forget the traditions of their ancestors.

SEE ALSO:
- ❖ Cosmology
- ❖ Dance
- ❖ Death Customs
- ❖ Fasting
- ❖ Medicine
- ❖ Medicine Bundle
- ❖ Ritual
- ❖ Sitting Bull
- ❖ Vision Quest

21

Shawnee

The traditional homelands of the Shawnee are in the Southeast, around the Cumberland Basin of the Tennessee River and on the Savannah River in South Carolina.

The tribe's name comes from the Algonquian word "Shawunogi," meaning "Southerners." Like their close linguistic relatives, the Sauk, Fox, and Kickapoo, they were a nomadic people. Sites of Shawnee villages have been found along rivers in Tennessee, Kentucky, Ohio, and Virginia. Perhaps no other tribe divided and moved so frequently.

ALLIES AND ENEMIES

Because they traveled regularly, the Shawnee often took on the customs of neighboring tribes. Like the northern Algonquians, they fished, hunted, and gathered wild foods. At the same time, they picked up the farming skills of the Southeastern tribes.

Although they were only a small tribe, the Shawnee formed alliances with many other groups. At various times they were allies of the Miami, Delaware, Ottawa, and Potawatomi.

Between 1689 and 1763 the Shawnee were allies of the French in the long wars with the English. It was largely due to opposition from the Shawnee and their allies that English expansion was limited. With help from the Miami, Potawatomi, Ojibway (Chippewa), and Ottawa, and supplied with arms and ammunition by the French, the Shawnee destroyed several English settlements. However, when the French were finally defeated by the English, the Shawnee lost their support.

BELOW: At the Battle of Tippecanoe on November 7, 1811, U.S. troops destroyed the Shawnee settlement of Prophetstown. Tenskwatawa, Tecumseh's brother, can be seen below wearing a pale robe with his arms raised.

After the wars the English promised the Shawnee land, but the governor of Virginia, Lord Dunmore, refused to honor the promise. Led by Chief Cornstalk, the Shawnee went to war with the Virginians but were defeated in 1774.

WAR WITH THE AMERICANS

The following year the American Revolutionary War began. The Shawnee supported the British and defeated some American armies but had their own settlements destroyed in 1780 and 1782 in retaliation by U.S. troops under George Rogers Clark. When the Americans won the war, the Shawnee once again had to resist an influx of new settlers onto their lands.

Along with the Delaware, Miami, and Ottawa, the Shawnee resisted these new incursions and fought and won several battles against the Americans. However, they were finally defeated by the U.S. Army at the Battle of Fallen Timbers in 1794.

A GREAT LEADER

Two Shawnee brothers—Tecumseh and Tenskwatawa—shared a vision of a united Native-American people. Tecumseh was probably the greatest Native-American leader of his time and worked tirelessly to unite the tribes at a crucial point in their history. But the hopes of Tecumseh and his brother ended when U.S. troops destroyed the Shawnee settlement at Tippecanoe in 1811.

Tecumseh's anger against the Americans was so great that he fought for the British during the

ABOVE:
This
painting depicts
Tenskwatawa,
Tecumseh's brother.

SEE ALSO:
❖ American
  Revolutionary
  War
❖ French and
  Indian War
❖ Indian Territory
❖ Tecumseh

War of 1812. He became a brigadier-general but was killed on October 5, 1813, at the Battle of the Thames.

Worn down by constant resistance to Europeans and Americans, the Shawnee divided. Some fled to Texas and Kansas, while others joined the Creek confederacy. A few bands went to the Indian Territory (part of present-day Oklahoma), but they settled in separate districts and lost any tribal group identity.

Shields

A Native-American warrior's shield was a vital piece of his war equipment, for it provided him with protection. Not only was his shield physically tough, but in the warrior's mind it also had supernatural qualities. Each warrior believed that his "medicine shield" contained the power of his guardian spirit, which would protect him from danger in battle.

BUILT TO BUFFER BLOWS

Native-American shields were generally round. Plains warriors made shields by smoking or heating layers of buffalo skin to shrink them and then stretching them thin. They padded them with hair, feathers, grass, or even paper. According to George Catlin, an artist who traveled among the Native Americans in the 1830s, warriors of some Plains tribes further toughened their shields with glue made by boiling buffalo hooves. Plains shields were tough enough to stop an arrow or a blow from a tomahawk, and skillfully handled, they could deflect a round from a low-powered firearm.

A Plains warrior took great care of his shield. He believed he could recharge its protective power by placing it on a stand and pointing it toward the sun. He would not usually let it touch the ground. However, one 19th-century Plains chief, Arapooish of the Crow tribe, had a shield that he rolled along the ground to predict the result of a coming battle. If the shield landed face upward, then Arapooish believed his war party would win.

Warriors often kept their shields in highly decorated cases. A Plains warrior usually also decorated his shield with likenesses of his guardian, or vision, spirit. It was this decoration that gave the shield its supernatural protective power. So if a warrior's guardian spirit was a buffalo, he might paint a buffalo's head on it.

When the Apache went to war, they tried to harness the powers of animal spirits that they revered. They sometimes painted pictures of these animals on their shields. One Apache shield, for example, bears images of a hummingbird, which the shield's owner believed could

ABOVE: Plains warriors often edged their shields with feathers. After the introduction of powerful rifles, against which traditional Plains warriors' shields offered no physical protection, warriors often carried small model shields, such as the one shown here, into battle.

lend him its speed, and a bat, which he thought could pass on its ability to hide and be hard to catch.

FROM SHIELDS TO SYMBOLS

Shields changed in size over the years. Before they acquired horses in the 18th century, Plains warriors carried shields that were about 3 feet (90 cm) across. However, shields this large were awkward on horseback, so Plains warriors changed to smaller ones of between 18 inches (45 cm) and 2 feet (60 cm) across.

The development of powerful firearms also influenced the size of Native-American warriors' shields. Realizing that their shields could not physically protect them from gunfire, warriors began to carry small, symbolic shields into battle. Like their full-sized shields, they decorated these models with likenesses of their guardian spirits and believed that they had the same supernatural protective powers. Sometimes warriors carried only their shield cover or even a lacework shield into battle.

LEFT: This shield belonged to a Plains warrior whose guardian spirit was a bear. Flying bullets are also depicted on this shield.

SEE ALSO:
- Apache
- Bows and Arrows
- Buffalo
- Crow
- Feathers for Warriors
- Firearms
- Horses
- Medicine
- Plains
- Tomahawk
- Warriors

Siouan Speakers

The Siouan language was spoken across a wide area, from the northern Great Lakes to Texas and Louisiana. The power of the many Siouan-speaking tribes balanced the aggression of the northern Algonquian and Iroquoian tribes.

Coming from such a large area, Siouan-speaking tribes had greatly varied cultures. Some were settled farmers; others, nomadic hunters. Some Siouan-speaking tribes were friendly toward each other, but many were deadly enemies.

There were Siouan speakers in the Southeast, including the Biloxi, Catawba, and Cheraw. But the greatest concentration of Siouan speakers was in the Plains and Woodland regions. The Woodland area encompassed the Sioux confederation and the Winnebago tribespeople. The Hidatsa and Mandan tribes lived in settled villages on the Upper Missouri River. The main Siouan speakers of the Plains were the Crow (relatives of the Hidatsa), the Assiniboine, Iowa, Kansa, Omaha, Osage, Oto, Ponca, Quapaw, and Dakota tribes.

SIOUX CONFEDERATION

The Sioux confederation was divided into three large groups. These were the eastern Dakota (Santee Sioux), central Nakota (Yankton Sioux), and western Lakota (Teton Sioux), each with a different dialect. "Dakota," "Nakota," and "Lakota" all mean "friendly ones" or "allies." The word "Sioux" is derived from an Ojibway (Chippewa) term *Nadowesioux*, meaning "adders" (signifying enemies). The Santee Sioux lived

RIGHT: Standing Bear was chief of the Ponca, one of the main Siouan-speaking tribes of the Plains.

SEE ALSO:
- Algonquian Speakers
- Assiniboine
- Buffalo
- Crow
- Homes
- Hunting
- Iroquoian Speakers
- Ojibway (Chippewa)
- Plains
- Sioux
- Southeast/ Florida
- Upper Missouri Tribes
- Woodland

around Lake Superior but were driven into modern-day Minnesota (Siouan for "many waters") in the 18th century by the Ojibway, who coveted their wild-rice lands.

The Yankton and Teton were driven farther still, onto the Plains, where their farming way of life ended and their days of nomadic buffalo-hunting began. On the Plains they lived in tepees—*tepee* means "they dwell" or "dwelling" in the Siouan language.

Siouan is typical of Native-American languages in that it can be used to express complicated ideas with a single word containing many separate, meaningful elements. Attaching other elements to verbs to form complex, one-word sentences is common in Siouan.

Sioux

Until the 18th century the Sioux lived in the Woodland region. There were three main groups: the Santee (eastern), Yankton (central), and Teton (western). The Teton comprised seven subtribes: the Blackfoot, Brule, Oglala, Sans Arcs, Minniconjou, Two-Kettle, and Hunkpapa. Surrounded by larger rival tribes—especially the Ojibway (Chippewa)—the Santee, Yankton, and Teton Sioux referred to themselves respectively as Dakota, Nakota, and Lakota, or "allies."

The name "Sioux" derives from an Ojibway word for "enemy." In the 18th century conflict with the Ojibway forced the Sioux, who together numbered about 25,000 at the time, to move onto the buffalo ranges of the Great Plains.

LIFE ON THE PLAINS

In the Woodland region the Sioux lived on deer, beans, and wild rice. On the Plains they lived a nomadic hunting lifestyle based on following the buffalo herds. The buffalo provided food, clothing, and shelter. The Sioux used nearly every part of the animal—skins for tepees and robes, hair for rope, sinews for thread, dung for fuel, and bladders for containers. They also traded, exchanging firearms and horses for tobacco and other goods from Great Lakes tribes.

The basic social and hunting unit of the Sioux was the band (an extended family group). Each band usually had more than one chief, respected men who offered advice but never gave orders. Important decisions at a tribal level were made by a council of many chiefs.

Polygamy (having more than one wife) was common for men, but a warrior could marry only after he had proved himself in battle and had enough horses to compensate his wife's father. Although they had no laws as such, the Sioux lived by a severe code of punishments for those who stepped out of line. Adultery by women was punished by disfigurement. Men disobeying

BELOW: Dressed here as a chief, Red Tomahawk was a Sioux member of the police force sent to arrest Sitting Bull in 1890. In the ensuing struggle he shot Sitting Bull dead.

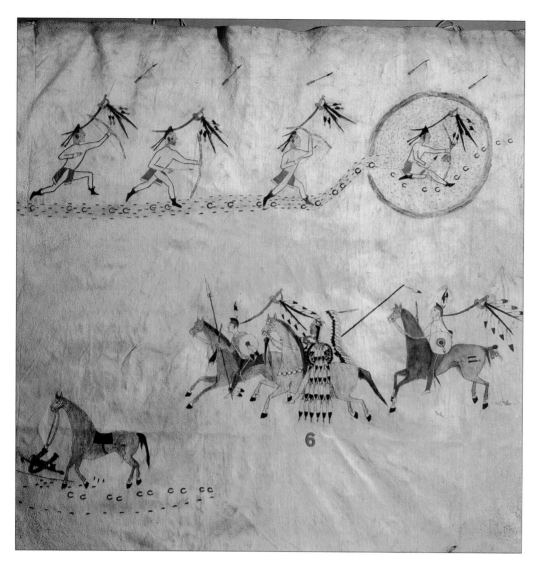

LEFT: This Sioux buffalo hide painting depicts a battle between Blackfoot and Sioux warriors.

the hunting regulations had their tepees and property destroyed. Old people too weak to travel with the band were simply left to die.

Men in Plains tribes acquired status through acts of bravery in battle, and Sioux warriors were particularly renowned for their courage. They wore specially cut feathers in their hair to signify their deeds. The bravest deed was counting coup—touching an enemy with a special stick.

The Sioux and the Cree were the only Plains tribes to consider scalping as a first-class war honor. Bringing home a scalp not only demonstrated a warrior's success, it was also believed to "capture" the dead man's spirit. The spirit would then accompany the victor as a companion when he himself died and traveled to the afterworld.

SPIRITUAL LIFE OF THE SIOUX

The Sioux believed in one all-powerful god, called Wakan Tanka, "the Great Spirit," who was present throughout the natural world.

A Sioux man's most sacred possession was his tobacco pipe, without which no ceremony could take place. Tribally owned pipes, or calumets, were smoked before going into battle, when making peace with an enemy, to bring rain, and to insure a successful buffalo hunt.

Young Sioux men often went on Vision Quests to seek direction from the spirit of an animal. They went off alone into the wilderness and fasted (went without food or water). They then called on the spirit for guidance. They also painted likenesses of these spirits on their war shields to protect themselves in battle.

FIGHTING FOR SURVIVAL

Of all the Great Plains tribes the Sioux most fiercely resisted incursions by white Americans on their lands. In 1851 the U.S. government signed the first Treaty of Fort Laramie with the Sioux and other tribes.

This treaty assigned boundaries to each tribe and arranged for forts and roads within their territories. But the peace was not to last, and a pattern of raiding developed as white settlers cut across Sioux lands, killing buffalo on their way to Oregon and California.

Throughout the 1860s matters worsened as settlers tried to open the Bozeman Trail—a route to the gold fields in the Rockies—through the Sioux's favorite hunting grounds in the Bighorn Mountains.

This was the trigger for Red Cloud's War (1865–1867). An Oglala Sioux chief, Red Cloud was the only Native American to lead a successful war against the U.S. Army. It ended with the second Fort Laramie treaty of 1868, which

BELOW: Painted by the 19th-century white American artist George Catlin, this scene depicts daily life in a Sioux village.

Fact File

In the 18th century the Sioux moved from the Woodland to the Plains.

LANGUAGE:	*Siouan*
AREA:	*Great Plains*
RESERVATION:	*North and South Dakota, Montana, and Nebraska.*
POPULATION:	*25,000 in 18th century; 40,000 today*
HOUSING:	*Tepees ("dwellings" in Siouan)*
EUROPEAN CONTACT:	*French settlers in the 18th century*
NEIGHBORS:	*Mandan, Crow, Cree, Cheyenne, Blackfoot, and Ojibway (Chippewa)*
LIFESTYLE:	*Nomadic buffalo hunters and warriors*
FOOD:	*Buffalo and other game animals*
CRAFTS:	*Bead embroidery, skinwork, and carving*

guaranteed southern Dakota to the Sioux and the scrapping of the trail. But when gold was discovered in the Black Hills in the mid-1870s, thousands of miners ignored the treaty and swarmed onto the Sioux reservation there with tacit army support. The conflict that followed ended with the Battle of Little Bighorn in 1876, where an alliance of Sioux, Arapaho, and Cheyenne warriors, led by Sitting Bull and Crazy Horse, famously surrounded and killed Lieutenant Colonel Custer and over 200 of his troops.

The spectacular victory was short-lived, and later that year the Sioux were forced to surrender and return to their reservations. Sitting Bull fled to Canada with several thousand followers but returned to the United States in 1881 and surrendered to the army.

In 1890 a movement known as the Ghost Dance religion spread across the Plains, promising Native Americans the destruction of white Americans, restocking of the Plains with buffalo, and the restoration of their deceased relatives. The movement took hold among the Sioux, who were starving on their reservations. But the government feared it might provoke another uprising and came to arrest Sitting Bull, who was killed during a scuffle. Finally, the U.S. Army's massacre of about 250 Sioux men, women, and children at Wounded Knee that year marked the end of all Sioux resistance.

BATTLE FOR SIOUX RIGHTS

Today there are over 40,000 Sioux, most of whom live on reservations. In recent years many Sioux have been active in the American Indian Movement (AIM), a civil rights organization that seeks the restoration of original tribal lands and better treatment of Native Americans in general. For example, in 1973 members of AIM occupied the town of Wounded Knee for 71 days and succeeded in provoking a U.S. Senate investigation into Native-American living conditions.

Sitting Bull

Sitting Bull led the Lakota Sioux of the northern Great Plains against U.S. Western expansion in the 1870s. He was born near the Grand River in South Dakota and belonged to the Hunkpapa band. As a child he was called Jumping Badger and fought his first battle, against the Crow, at the age of 14. After another battle in 1857 he earned the name Tatanka Yotanka—usually translated as "Sitting Bull." The full meaning of Tatanka Yotanka—"Buffalo bull sitting, unmovable, on his haunches"—more accurately reflects his character.

Sitting Bull's reputation for courage and wisdom grew. He was a shaman and about 1868 became head of the Lakota. He is best known for leading the force that defeated Lieutenant Colonel George A. Custer at the Battle of the Little Bighorn in 1876.

WAR WITH THE U.S.

The Treaty of Fort Laramie, signed in 1868 at the end of Red Cloud's War, was supposed to protect Lakota lands—including the sacred Black Hills of South Dakota. But as more and more settlers came to the region, violence broke out again. When Custer's 1874 expedition confirmed the discovery of gold in the Black Hills, the conflict rapidly escalated. Despite the treaty of 1868, prospectors poured into the area, and when the U.S. government failed to buy the land from the Lakota, it ordered their removal to reservations by January 1876.

Under the leadership of Sitting Bull many Lakota, Cheyenne, and Arapaho refused to relocate to

ABOVE: Sitting Bull (left) toured with Buffalo Bill Cody's (right) Wild West Show in the 1880s, when this photograph was taken.

reservations, and in the spring of 1876 troops under generals Terry, Gibbon, and Crook converged on them. Sitting Bull had a vision in which the troops fell into the Sioux camp like grasshoppers and were then destroyed: it was to prove

HIS LATER YEARS

After Little Bighorn Sitting Bull fled to Canada, but the near extinction of the Lakota's main food source—buffalo—through overhunting caused his people great hardship. He eventually surrendered and agreed to settle on a reservation, but he was put in prison at Fort Randall for two years despite the promise of a pardon.

Sitting Bull returned to the Standing Rock reservation in 1883 but was allowed to leave again in 1885 to perform in Buffalo Bill's Wild West Show (probably because the government felt his presence on the reservation was a bad influence). However, the 50 dollars per week Sitting Bull earned in the show could not overcome his dislike of nonnative lifestyles and values, and he soon returned to the reservation.

In the late 1880s the Ghost Dance movement, led by a Paiute named Wovoka, was causing unrest on the Lakota reservations. On December 15, 1890, reservation police tried to arrest Sitting Bull, fearing he might use this new movement to inspire a Lakota rebellion. A struggle began and shots were fired. In the resulting fight Sitting Bull was killed.

remarkably accurate. When Custer's Seventh Cavalry stumbled across a camp of Lakota and Cheyenne on the Little Bighorn River, he rashly attacked without waiting for support. His men were wiped out by a much larger force led by Sitting Bull, Crazy Horse, and Gall.

ABOVE: This 19th-century illustration depicts Custer's "last stand" (the final moments of his defeat) at the Little Bighorn on June 25, 1876.

SEE ALSO:
- Black Hills
- Buffalo
- Crazy Horse
- Disenfranchisement
- Ghost Dance
- Little Bighorn
- Plains
- Red Cloud's War
- Siouan Speakers
- Sioux
- Treaties
- Wounded Knee
- Wovoka

Soto, Hernando de

Hernando de Soto was a Spanish explorer who is famous for his pioneering expedition through the southeastern United States. Born into a noble but poor family in 1500, he followed his patron, Pedro Arias de Avila, to Central America in 1519. In the 1530s he served under the infamous conquistador, or conqueror, Pizzaro during his conquest of the Incas in Peru. Enriched in both reputation and treasure, de Soto was granted the governorship of Cuba and given a royal warrant to explore the little-known land of Florida.

GREED FOR GOLD

Landing in Tampa Bay in May 1539 with 600 men, de Soto set out to explore regions to the north in search of gold, which would bring him wealth and fame. Traveling north, he demanded supplies and information from Native-American tribes and seized their chiefs if they did not cooperate. From Apalachee Bay he sent a party along the Gulf Coast and then headed inland through Georgia to South Carolina, where Native Americans gave him a gift of pearls. Spurred on by false stories of gold, de Soto then traveled through North Carolina, Georgia, Tennessee, and Alabama, where he met his first serious resistance at the Battle of Mabila.

In May 1541 he reached the Mississippi River. He then journeyed into Arkansas and possibly Oklahoma and Missouri before returning through Louisiana a disappointed man. Exhausted by his efforts, de Soto died on the Mississippi near present-day Ferriday on

ABOVE: De Soto, depicted in this drawing, was probably the first European to see the mighty Mississippi River.

May 21, 1542. His party had searched a quarter of a million square miles (650,000 sq. km) and found no gold. By the time it straggled into Tampico in Mexico in 1543, half the party had died. Few were in a hurry to return to the southeastern U.S.

SEE ALSO:
- ❖ Coronado, Francisco de
- ❖ Cortés, Hernando
- ❖ Natchez
- ❖ Southeast/ Florida
- ❖ Timucua

RIGHT: Many tribes of the Southeast used a concoction called "black drink" before the start of a ceremony. It was believed that the drink purified the participants of the ceremony. Here a shaman is depicted pouring black drink onto a fire to cleanse his tribe.

The Southeast forms a vast area that was home to dozens of tribes and powerful confederacies. It is bordered by the Atlantic to the east, semitropical Florida and the Gulf of Mexico to the south and southwest, the Mississippi River to the west, and the Virginia–North Carolina coastal plain to the north.

This wet, humid, and densely wooded region was once home to North America's most highly civilized tribes, the Mound Builders, who were active west of the Appalachian Mountains between 1000 B.C. and A.D. 1500. They built thousands of mounds and earthworks during this period. The Mound Builders traded with, and may have been influenced by, the great temple-building civilizations of ancient Mexico. There were two major cultures: Woodland to the north and Mississippian to the south.

IMPRESSIVE SETTLEMENTS

Before the arrival of Europeans these peoples had a well-developed farming tradition, cultivating gourds, squashes, seed plants, beans, and corn. The ready availability of raw materials such as timber enabled them to build impressive towns and villages. Characteristically, these were defensively palisaded, or fenced, and their centerpieces were flat-topped mounds for ceremonial temples. Some towns were large ceremonial centers, the best known being Cahokia, with dozens of mounds. Cahokia may have had a population of 30,000 at its peak.

These Southeast societies were hierarchical. Their elites of priests or hereditary leaders wielded absolute power. Keenly aware of their status and power, they ruled tribute-levying chiefdoms—often of many villages—until the Spanish conquistadors, or conquerors, Ponce de León and Hernando de Soto arrived in the 16th century. However, war, internal tensions, and diseases introduced by Europeans soon took an irreversible toll.

Little is known about most of the peoples of the Southeast before they were decimated. One thing that we do know is that many of them were heavily tattooed and had pierced bodies. The most prominent groups were the Alabama, Biloxi, Caddo, Calusa, Catawba, Chakchiuma, Cherawa, Cherokee, Chickasaw, Chitimacha, Choctaw, Chowanac, Coushatta, Creek, Houma, Natchez, Quapaw, Seminole, Timucua, Tunica, and Yamasee.

They waged war on each other because of rivalries, for enrichment, for honor—and for captives for slavery, sacrifice, and cannibalism. These latter practices revolted the staunchly Catholic Spaniards who made the first recorded European contacts following Ponce de León's arrival in Florida in 1513. But it took the Spanish time to stop them.

Warfare to force compliance and assert dominance was common, so there was resistance to settlement and conquest. But the European pressure—from all the major

BELOW: The Pre-Contact peoples of the Southeast had rich and diverse cultures. This finely carved wooden pelican originates from Key Marco in Florida and is from the period A.D. 800 to A.D. 1400.

powers over time: Britain, France, Spain, and then the new United States—coupled with the terrible epidemics of disease, resulted in the decimation of the tribes.

EVERYDAY SOUTHEAST LIFE

Homes varied, but many were conical and thatched with grass or bark. Others were cabins made of wood and built on piles that raised them above the damp or swampy ground or were cool, open-sided "chickee" huts. The people practiced a great deal of farming and fishing, with the rich forests, swamps, and saltwater marshes providing all kinds of game for

LEFT: This early photograph is of Key West Billy, a member of the Seminole tribe.

hunters. Harvests and associated festivals were the centerpiece of the ritual year, notably the Green Corn ceremonies and dances.

The best-known Southeast tribes are the so-called Five Civilized Tribes (the Cherokee, Choctaw, Chickasaw, Creek, and Seminole). Many of the remnants of the other, once great peoples of the region may live on in their ranks.

The defining event for them was President Andrew Jackson's brutal policy of forced relocation following his Indian Removal Act of 1830—the infamous "Trail of Tears." One-quarter of all Cherokee died during this march over hundreds of miles of harsh terrain. The removal took place despite the Supreme Court ruling in favor of the Cherokee and upholding the principle of tribal sovereignty.

STRUGGLE FOR SURVIVAL

Even so, small groups managed to resist the policy and remain in their homelands, such as the eastern Cherokee of Qualla reservation in the Great Smoky Mountains.

But most of their descendants now live in Oklahoma, their culture massively diminished. Lower Creek emigrants to Florida had become the Seminole, or "separatists," and it was they who were the first to resist Jackson's designs when he waged war against them as an army officer in 1818. His second attempt to oust them from Florida in 1835 was costly because of determined Seminole resistance that lasted years. It enabled some of them at least to survive in the Everglades—where they still live today.

Southwest

The Southwest is a large semi-desert area. Centered on New Mexico and Arizona, the region extends south into northern Mexico, east to Texas, and north into Utah and Colorado. Although the climate of the Southwest is extremely dry, the region has been home to various Native-American tribes for over 2,000 years. The early occupants of the region—the Anasazi, Hohokam, and Mogollon—survived the arid climate by channeling river flood waters.

They grew corn, beans, squash, and cotton and were able to harvest two crops a year. Their basic farming methods are still practiced today by their descendants and other tribes of the region.

SOUTHWEST PEOPLES

The Anasazi and Mogollon lived in dwellings made from adobe (sun-dried bricks of mud and straw) and are the ancestors of the modern Pueblo tribes. The Anasazi and Mogollon were peaceful, settled peoples who traded with groups throughout the area and beyond.

The Hohokam, ancestors of the modern Papago and Pima tribespeople, lived in cane-and-brush shelters along the river banks. They spent much of the year hunting, although later, under the influence of the Anasazi, they built permanent dwellings and had large fields of crops.

The Pueblo of the Rio Grande, together with the Zuni and Hopi, are probably best known for their mulitchambered adobe dwellings—the first apartment buildings. They are also known for their weaving,

BELOW: This photograph from about 1900 shows a member of the Zia tribe of New Mexico performing a war dance.

pottery, and the cultivation of corn. These tribes have a rich religious ceremonial tradition, often linked to rain, fertility, and farming.

LIFESTYLE OF THE PUEBLO

During the 16th century the arrival of the Spanish in the region brought about changes in Pueblo lifestyle. For example, many Pueblo tribespeople were converted to Catholicism and helped build

mission churches in their villages. However, the Pueblo did not give up all of their traditional beliefs. Today they still worship kachinas—ancestral deities that the Pueblo believe watch over the tribe and insure its survival. The kachinas are represented in the form of dolls given to children and as masks worn by dancers during ceremonies.

The Pueblo are made up of four language groups: Tanoan, Keresan, Zunian, and Uto-Aztecan. They are also divided into two regional groups—the Eastern and Western Pueblo. The Eastern is the largest of the two groups; and although both cultures are based on farming, the Eastern group depends more heavily on irrigation.

THE PAPAGO AND PIMA
The Papago and Pima live near the Eastern and Western Pueblo, with whom they are friendly. Both tribes are Uto-Aztecan speakers and are

linguistically related to the Chemehuevi, Ute, and Paiute tribes living in Utah and Colorado.

Unlike the Pueblo who lived in permanent villages, the Papago and Pima were seminomadic, spending spring and summer in temporary villages made up of cane-and-brush shelters built near rivers. During these warmer months the Papago and Pima tended their fields. However, during winter they moved into more sheltered locations in the mountains where they hunted deer and small game. The two tribes are also excellent basketmakers.

The Papago and Pima sometimes came into conflict over resources with more warlike farmers in the region—usually Hokan speakers. These groups were divided into the Upper Yuma (Havasupai, Walapai, and Yavapai), who combined farming with gathering berries and roots, and the Lower Yuma (Cochimi, Cocopa, Cocomaricopa,

BELOW: The Pueblo building in this photograph is made from adobe. It is in Taos Pueblo, New Mexico.

LEFT: This detail from an Apache warrior's cloak shows a painting of an Apache "Kan," or god.

Halchidhoma, Yuma, and Mohave), who lived along the Colorado River and its tributaries.

INVASION OF THE SOUTHWEST

The relatively peaceful world of the Southwest was disrupted in the late 15th century by the arrival of Athapascan-speaking Apache groups.

These nomadic hunter-gatherers had migrated to the Southwest from the far north. They adopted many Southwest customs and ideas but did not become farmers. Instead, the Apache supplemented their hunting-gathering activities by raiding the Pueblo and other tribes in the area.

In the early 16th century the Southwest was disrupted by Spanish conquistadors who tried to dominate the tribes of the region. However, the

SEE ALSO:

- Anasazi
- Apache
- Basketry
- Chaco Canyon
- Cochise
- Corn
- Geronimo
- Hohokam
- Hopi
- Kachina
- Kiva
- Mangas Coloradas
- Masks
- Mesa Verde
- Mogollon
- Navajo
- Papago and Pima
- Pueblo
- Rugs and Blankets
- Zuni

Apache provided fierce resistance to both the Spanish and the U.S. settlers who came to the area later. During the 19th century the Apache produced great military chiefs including Geronimo, Cochise, and Mangas Coloradas, who spent years preventing U.S. troops from securing the region.

The Navajo—who are related to the Apache—are well known for their finely woven blankets and rugs. In the 16th century the Spanish introduced sheep and goats to the region, and the Navajo learned how to weave from the Pueblo. The Navajo are also famed for their silver and turquoise jewelry.

THE SOUTHWEST TODAY

The Pueblo were greatly affected by Spanish, Mexican, and U.S. wars, invasions, and dispossession, as well as by the raids of the Apache and Navajo. However, the Pueblo have managed to retain many of their original customs and beliefs, remaining one of the most traditional tribes. Some Pueblo still live in adobe villages that have been continuously occupied for the past 1,000 years, and many of their ceremonies are closed to outsiders.

The more progressive Navajo prospered in the Southwest and are today the largest tribe in the United States. They make huge amounts of high-quality weaving and jewelry.

The lifestyles of the Papago and Pima have changed significantly. Today many members of the two tribes earn their living by raising cattle. Tribal income also comes from mining leases on their reservations. The Apache also earn tribal income from leasing rights to minerals and timber on their lands.

Spain, Wars with

After the Genoese explorer Christopher Columbus landed in America in 1492, Spanish conquistadors, or conquerors, quickly began colonizing various islands in the Caribbean. Within 30 years they had moved onto the North American mainland and subdued the rich and powerful Aztec rulers of Mexico. By the end of the 16th century the Spanish empire had spread north to include much of present-day Arizona, New Mexico, Texas, and Florida.

DEADLY NEW DISEASES

In the process millions of Native Americans died because the conquistadors inevitably brought with them from Europe diseases, such as smallpox, that previously were unknown in the Americas. Native Americans had no immunity to these diseases, and dreadful epidemics followed that in some cases killed whole populations.

The Spanish also made cruel and ruthless use of their superior military technology. Native Americans had no firearms and no knowledge of metalwork to compete with the Spaniards' swords and body armor. Horses were also a new and terrifying sight for Native Americans, who had no answer to Spanish cavalry charges. With these advantages a few hundred Spaniards defeated native armies that numbered many thousands of warriors.

The first large-scale conquest began when Hernando Cortés led an expedition to Mexico in 1519.

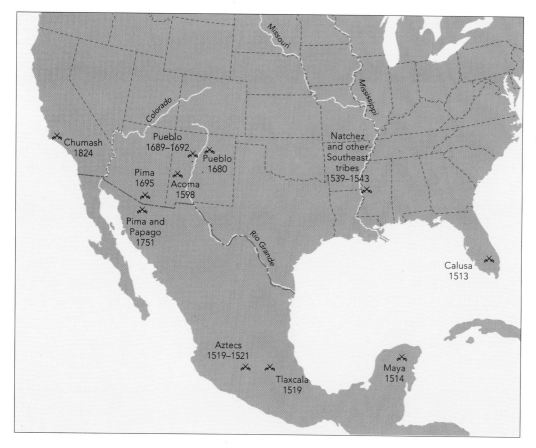

Chumash
1824

Pueblo
1689–1692

Pueblo
1680

Pima
1695

Acoma
1598

Pima and
Papago
1751

Natchez
and other
Southeast
tribes
1539–1543

Calusa
1513

Aztecs
1519–1521

Tlaxcala
1519

Maya
1514

LEFT: This map shows the main battles that occurred between the Spanish and specific Native-American tribes.

The Aztec ruler Montezuma II led a huge, powerful, and warlike empire, but it seems he believed Cortés was an incarnation of an Aztec god and did little to hinder his advance. Cortés was quickly established in the Aztec capital of Tenochtitlán (now Mexico City) but had to leave soon after to defeat a Spanish rival. When he returned, he had to mount a full-scale siege to recapture the city, which he did in August 1521 after a devastating smallpox epidemic wiped out many of the defenders. Montezuma II died in the fighting, although no one knows whether he was killed by the Spanish or by his own people.

FAILURE IN FLORIDA

The first known Spanish incursion into what is now the United States was led by Juan Ponce de León in 1513. Ponce de León had already commanded the conquest of Puerto Rico, but when he landed in Florida, he was soon driven off by the native people. He returned in 1521 with plans to establish a colony but was wounded in battle and died soon after. Permanent European settlement in Florida had to wait until Pedro Menéndez de Aviles built a fort at St. Augustine in 1565.

After de León there were other Spanish expeditions, some into the heart of North America. From 1539 to 1542 Hernando de Soto led an army from Florida through Georgia and then west as far as Oklahoma, before returning down the Mississippi River to the sea. De Soto died near the end of his march, but not before he and his 600 men had fought numerous battles and

plundered, tortured, and enslaved many of the native peoples they met on their journey. In one battle near present-day Mobile they killed 11,000 of their enemies, according to one eyewitness.

FRUITLESS SEARCH FOR GOLD

Another expedition traveled north overland from Mexico about the same time. In 1540 Francisco de Coronado set out to investigate rumors of vast wealthy cities and great gold reserves. By 1541 he and his men reached as far north as Kansas, fighting several battles with the Zuni and other peoples of New Mexico and the Rio Grande Valley on the way. They found no gold, and the discouraging report Coronado made on his return helped prevent further Spanish moves into this region for another half century. However, in 1598 and 1599 Juan de Oñate conquered the Pueblo peoples of the Rio Grande Valley and began a long period of tyrannical Spanish rule that was to last until the 1800s.

ABOVE: As this painting depicts, when the Spanish attacked native villages, they often burned them down and killed everyone.

SEE ALSO:
- Aztecs
- Columbus, Christopher
- Coronado, Francisco de
- Cortés, Hernando de
- Epidemics
- Extinction
- Firearms
- Horses
- Pueblo
- Soto, Hernando de
- Southeast/ Florida
- Tenochtitlán
- Zuni

Sterilization

Sterilization—a medical procedure that ends a woman's ability to have children—was a controversial subject for Native Americans during the 1970s and 1980s. For some Native-American women not having children seemed a practical way to relieve the economic strain of the time. They also believed that it would give them independence, the freedom to seek employment, and the opportunity to gain self-reliance.

Those most likely to undergo sterilization were young reservation women who relied on state assistance, were poorly educated, and were single mothers with young children. In reservations where up to 70 percent of the local population might be unemployed, sterilization was viewed as one solution to the local economic and social problems. Young Native-American girls who had not yet reached puberty were often sterilized to stop them having children in the future.

FEDERAL RESPONSIBILITY

Incredibly, in an age of modern health care, many Native Americans, especially those in poor rural reservation areas, did not have access to the resources of large hospitals. Instead, they were often dependent on an underfunded public health service run by poorly paid, overworked, and at times undertrained staff. Native Americans generally referred to this as the Indian Health Service, since it is guaranteed by treaties.

Although the hospital performing the operation had to obtain consent forms directly from the women being sterilized, these women did not always understand the forms that they were signing. Also it is uncertain if the consequences of sterilization had been fully explained to them beforehand.

In the early 1990s information and support services supplied by Native-American Women's Action Groups and closer cooperation between tribal representatives and health service officials began to examine ways in which unnecessary operations, such as sterilization, could be avoided.

ABOVE: This protest against the sterilization of Native-American women took place in 1980.

SEE ALSO:
- Children
- Education
- Reservations
- Women

Sun Dance

The Sun Dance was an annual ceremony for many of the Great Plains tribes. Its name comes from a Siouan ritual called "Gazing at the Sun," but it had little to do with sun worship. It took place in the fall, when the nomadic bands or family groups of hunters gathered as tribes to celebrate and to perform rituals that they believed renewed the world. It was an occasion for socializing with other bands, arranging marriages, feasting, dancing, and holding a great buffalo hunt.

Although the Sun Dance originated with the Sioux, many other tribes had similar renewal rituals and adopted aspects of the Sioux Sun Dance. The most important of these was that the participants danced to drumbeats and songs that they believed matched the natural rhythm of the universe and encouraged growth and fertility.

They used a buffalo skull as an altar to emphasize their link with the animal on which their survival depended. They also put up a pole—a specially cut tree—at the center of a lodge to express their connection with nature and to pay respect to all growing things.

SKEWERS AND THONGS

European and white American observers in the 19th century noted that some Sun Dancers attached themselves to the pole with thongs tied to skewers inserted through the skin on their chests. By fasting (going without food or drink) for four days and then painfully tearing themselves free from the skewers— leaving scars they would bear for the rest of their lives—these Sun Dancers hoped to obtain a vision, or dream, that would benefit themselves and their people.

BELOW: A Sioux, photographed about 1880, undergoes ritual self-mutilation on the fourth day of a Sun Dance.

LEFT: This bison-hide painting from the 1880s shows Plains people, probably Sioux, taking part in a Sun Dance. A cross indicates the influence of Christianity on Plains culture.

Most Sun Dancers who suffered this ordeal did so because of a personal crisis—often the death of a wife, husband, or child. They felt the pain would ease their sorrow.

White observers exaggerated the importance of self-torture in the Sun Dance, and the U.S. government regarded it as a barbaric ceremony that prevented tribes from adopting Christianity. The government therefore banned Sun Dances in 1881. Many Great Plains tribes continued to hold them in secret, however, until in 1934 the ban was officially lifted by the government.

Many Great Plains tribes still hold Sun Dances, both as sacred rituals of spiritual renewal and as statements of tribal pride and identity. Sun Dances today are usually held far from the public gaze, in remote reservation areas thought to be full of spiritual power. Leonard Peltier, a leading member of the radical American Indian Movement, took part in a Sun Dance on the Lakota Sioux reservation at Rosebud, South Dakota, in 1973. He said afterward, "I felt great for weeks… feeling that my body had been thoroughly cleansed inside and out."

SEE ALSO:
❖ Buffalo
❖ Dance
❖ Fasting
❖ Hunting
❖ Marriage
❖ Medicine
❖ Movies
❖ Music
❖ Plains
❖ Reservations
❖ Ritual
❖ Sioux
❖ Vision Quest

Sweat Lodge

RIGHT: Three men pose outside a sweat lodge in a Crow village in Montana.

Sweat lodges are small steam-filled shelters much like saunas. They were originally used by shamans (medicine men and women) and ordinary members of Plains tribes in ceremonies undertaken to make contact with the spirit powers. The idea was that by sweating profusely, they purified their bodies. This then allowed them to experience visions. Today sweat lodges are popular with Native Americans everywhere.

SIMPLE STRUCTURES

Traditionally, sweat lodges were usually constructed out of animal skins or blankets draped over a wooden framework. Sometimes they were made simply by draping canvas over the branches of a cottonwood tree. The ease and speed with which they could be

put up and taken down reflects the fact they were used by nomads who needed to keep on the move.

To maintain a constant cloud of steam inside a sweat lodge, the shaman regularly poured water over rocks that had been heated in a fire pit. Those who sought a vision sat bare-chested and bare-legged inside the lodge and scraped the sweat off their skin with sticks.

Wallace Black Elk, a 20th-century spiritual leader of the Lakota Sioux, explained the importance of sweat lodges to his people as follows: "The sweat lodge is made of from 12 to 16 young willows, and these too have a lesson to teach us, for in the fall their leaves die and return to earth, but in the spring they come to life again. So too men die, but live again in the real world of Wakan-Tanka [Great Spirit], where

there is nothing but the spirits of all things, and this true life we may know here on earth if we purify our bodies and minds…"

The sweat lodge has an important spiritual significance in that it combines the four basic elements of Plains Native-American cosmology: fire, air, water, and earth (in the form of the rocks). The darkness inside the lodge represents the lack of knowledge that people have of the ways of the spirit world. This is a recurring theme in many Native-American religions—as seen in the the *kivas* of the Pueblo people of the Southwest and the so-called shaking tents used by the Ojibway (Chippewa) of the Great Lakes.

Sweat lodges were also used by the Menomini, Potawatomi, Ojibway, and Ottawa peoples of the Great Lakes region in naming ceremonies. The parents of an infant who was ready to be named

sat inside a sweat lodge until the child's name was revealed to them by the spirit powers in a vision.

SECRET SWEAT LODGES

Like many traditional Native-American religious practices, such as peyote, sweat-lodge ceremonies were banned by the U.S. government following the final defeat of Native Americans in 1890 in the massacre at Wounded Knee. Native Americans continued to use sweat lodges in secret, however. The ban was not lifted until 1934, after which sweat lodges quickly became popular once again.

During the 1960s and 1970s sweat-lodge ceremonies were frequently held by Native Americans who were striving to reassert their tribal rights and traditional cultures. Since the 1980s sweat lodges have also become popular with some nonnative Americans.

SEE ALSO:
❖ Children
❖ Crow
❖ Kiva
❖ Medicine
❖ Ojibway (Chippewa)
❖ Peyote
❖ Plains
❖ Pueblo
❖ Shamanism
❖ Sioux
❖ Vision Quest
❖ Wounded Knee

Taboos

In its widest sense a taboo is a ban on a particular action that is believed to be repugnant or in some way harmful to society as a whole. For example, in most cultures around the world it is taboo to eat human flesh or to have sexual relations with a close relative such as a brother or sister. Such actions are usually forbidden by law, but many minor taboos are kept by people even though they are not officially laid down by law.

NATIVE-AMERICAN TABOOS

In traditional Native-American cultures many actions were considered taboo because they might disrupt the correct relationship between the natural world and the power of the spirit world. If broken, such a taboo could result in severe physical or emotional damage to the person who broke it, to members of his or her family, or even to his or her descendants a hundred years later. It could then be fixed only by performing certain ritual actions that restored the balance of powers between the spirit world and the human world.

Such Native-American taboos covered a range of actions. For example, among the Iglulik Inuit of Arctic Canada the list of taboos included: eating the breast of a caribou in summer; touching game within a certain period after recovering from an illness; combing one's hair shortly after giving birth; wearing clothes made of caribou hide while preparing ammunition for a hunt; removing hair from the skin of a spotted seal; and using the lamp of a dead person.

TABOOS ABOUT CHILDBIRTH

Many traditional Native-American taboos were connected to the female menstrual cycle and giving birth. This is a list of Cheyenne taboos put together by a white scholar in 1904: young men could not eat or drink from dishes or pots used by a menstruating woman; a menstruating woman could not touch any weapon, shield, or medicine bundle; a menstruating woman could not ride

BELOW: This carved and painted figure of a shaman in ritual robes and a headdress comes from the Northwest Coast. Shamans often attributed various ills and misfortunes to the breaking of specific tribal taboos.

stallions, only mares; a menstruating woman could not enter a lodge containing a medicine bundle. Isolation in a special lodge was imposed on most tribal women each month when they were menstruating. Inuit women were also required to give birth alone in a separate hut or tent. A man of a Woodland tribe had to fast (go without food) for four days after his wife gave birth.

DEATH AND TABOOS

Other traditional Native-American taboos were associated with death and the world of the dead. Among the Navajo the husband of a woman who died could not become involved in an emotional relationship with another woman for one year after the death of his wife. He was not even allowed to court a woman for one year.

Other death taboos related to the belongings of the deceased. Among the Washo people of the Great Basin a dwelling in which a death occurred was abandoned or even burned down. People of the Native-American tribes of the Northwest Coast had to break a hole through the wall of a house in which a person had died to remove the body: on no account was the body to be taken through the door. Native-American burial grounds in general were taboo places, especially those platform graves of the Plains peoples.

BELOW: Burial grounds such as this one, which has wooden figures representing the dead, were taboo places for most Native Americans.

HUNTING TABOOS

A great many Native-American taboos related to hunting. Luck is a powerful factor in the pursuit of game—a sudden noise near the quarry, caused by another animal or by a rival hunting party, could easily make the difference between success and failure. To avoid such bad luck, it was essential not to break certain taboos.

Since Native Americans believed that the animals they hunted were powerful spirit beings, one of the most important taboos among hunting tribes was not to treat their prey disrespectfully. Bragging about one's ability to catch animals risked incurring a period of bad luck for the tribe's hunters, since it implied that a mere human was wiser than a supernatural being.

After a successful hunt a prayer or chant might be recited over the body of the dead animal. This gave thanks to the spirit being that was present in the animal for allowing itself to be caught and asked it to return in a new form so that a future hunt could be successful, too. The Mistassini Cree of Canada placed the bones of a butchered bear on a raised platform similar to the kind used by many tribes of the Plains for their own human dead.

This was a mark of respect to insure that scavengers did not scatter the remains. The Apache believed that eating a deer's tongue would offend the spirit of deer.

There were many other taboos among Native Americans relating to diverse activities, but all connected with the harmony between the natural and the spirit worlds. For example, the Apache believed that if a person leaned against a tree that had been struck by lightning, he or she would fall ill. Among the Pima people if a person made fun of someone with a mental disability, he or she risked having the same fate befall his or her own child or one of his or her relatives.

ABOVE: This stone pipe belonged to a shaman of the Cherokee, one of the so-called Five Civilized Tribes. The shaman used it in a ceremony after someone broke a taboo to restore harmony with the spirit world.

SEE ALSO:

- Apache
- Basin and Plateau
- Birth Customs
- Cheyenne
- Cree
- Death Customs
- Fasting
- Five Civilized Tribes
- Hunting
- Inuit
- Medicine
- Medicine Bundle
- Navajo
- Northwest Coast
- Papago and Pima
- Plains
- Shamanism
- Women
- Woodland

Tanoan Speakers

The Kiowa–Tanoan language family is distantly related to the more widely spoken Uto-Aztecan language. Together they represent one of the great language groups in North America—Aztec–Tanoan.

Speakers in this language group cover a large geographical area. They include tribes from the northern Plateau, the southern Plains, the Southwest, and Mexico and Central America. Aztec–Tanoan is related to Nahuatlan–Aztec and Mayan. Kiowa–Tanoan itself is based in Oklahoma and New Mexico.

The Kiowa–Tanoan group consists of the Tanoan-speaking southern Plains Kiowa tribe in Oklahoma and the Tiwa, Tewa, and Towa languages of the eastern Pueblo Indians of New Mexico. The Pueblo Indians have 11 Tanoan-speaking pueblos: six Tewa pueblos (Nambe, Pojoaque, San Ildefonso, San Juan, Santa Clara, and Tesuque), four Tiwa (Isleta, Picurís, Sandía, and Taos), and one Towa (Jémez). There is a 12th Tanoan group— a Tewa-speaking Western Pueblo group at Hano in Hopi territory.

KIOWA AND COMANCHE

The Kiowa tribe of warrior-horsemen ranged the southern Plains and were among the last of the Native-American tribes to succumb to the growing power of the United States.

The Kiowa lived closely with the Comanche, even though they spoke different languages, and the two tribes often raided as far south as Mexico for horses. Today there are about 11,000 speakers of Kiowa–Tanoan languages.

ABOVE: This photograph from about 1900 shows a Tanoan-speaking girl from the Nambe pueblo in the Southwest.

SEE ALSO:
- ❖ Aztecs
- ❖ Comanche
- ❖ Horses
- ❖ Kiowa
- ❖ Plains
- ❖ Pueblo
- ❖ Southwest
- ❖ Uto-Aztecan

Taos

BELOW: The present occupants of Taos pueblo have added windows and doors to their traditional houses. Originally, the only openings were in the roofs, for protection against enemies.

Taos pueblo lies in a valley below the Taos Mountains in northern New Mexico. The site has been occupied for almost 1,000 years. Along with Acoma village in western New Mexico and the mesas of the Hopi reservation in northeastern Arizona, it is one of the oldest continuously inhabited settlements in the United States.

The first inhabitants of Taos were Tiwa-speaking peoples who may originally have traveled across the Great Plains from the east. These Native Americans came to play a major part in the Pueblo culture found across present-day Arizona and New Mexico.

Being one of the northernmost pueblos in New Mexico, Taos was one of the few settlements to survive the arrival of the Spanish conquistadors, or conquerors, early in the 16th century. However, when the Spanish reconquered the area following the unsuccessful Pueblo

Rebellion of 1680, the Taos pueblo was almost completely destroyed by the invading forces.

A HISTORY OF REBELLION

In 1837 Taos Native Americans beheaded their Mexican governor. In 1847, after the area was taken over by the United States, Taos was deeply implicated in the rebellion against its first U.S. governor, Charles Bent, and was severely repressed. Over 150 inhabitants died when the U.S. Army besieged and set ablaze the pueblo's church.

Only two pueblo buildings, Hlauuma and Hlaukwima, built on either side of the Río Pueblo de Taos, now survive. These date from

ABOVE: The people of Taos still use traditional clay dome-shaped ovens for baking.

the 18th century and are two-story "apartment" houses built in the traditional style—although access has been improved by adding doors to the original rooftop ladders. Although there are no toilets, running water, or electricity, 100 Native Americans continue to live in these houses, while a further 2,000 live in modern houses on the surrounding reservation.

SEE ALSO:
- ❖ Acoma Village
- ❖ Homes
- ❖ Hopi
- ❖ Pueblo
- ❖ Pueblo Rebellion
- ❖ Reservations
- ❖ Southwest

Tecumseh

Tecumseh was a Shawnee leader who sought to forge an alliance of all Native-American tribes east of the Mississippi River against rapid U.S. expansion following the American Revolutionary War (1775–1783). He was an eloquent orator, a brilliant diplomat, and an inspirational war leader.

Tecumseh was born in 1768 in the village of Piqua near Springfield, Ohio. Armed struggle against the white settlers was part of his life from childhood. His father, a Shawnee chief, was killed while fighting settlers at Point Pleasant in 1774. As a young man Tecumseh helped defeat General Harmer at Fort Wayne in 1790 and General St. Clare on the Wabash River in 1791. But these victories could not stop the flow of new settlers into Ohio, and after their own defeat by General Anthony Wayne at the Battle of Fallen Timbers in 1794 the power of the Great Lakes tribes seemed to have been crushed.

NEW CENTURY, NEW HOPE
In the early 19th century Tecumseh gave renewed hope, direction, and purpose to the Great Lakes tribes, continuing the struggle of Pontiac two generations earlier.

Before 1776 the British had tried—often unsuccessfully—to prevent white colonial settlement west of the Appalachian Mountains, but after the American Revolutionary War the floodgates were opened. A huge influx of settlers came down the Ohio, Allegheny, and Monongahela rivers into Native-American lands in the Midwest. Together with his twin

ABOVE: In the War of 1812 Tecumseh sided with the British, who made him a brigadier-general in charge of all the Native-American forces.

brother, Tenskwatawa (a shaman also called "the Prophet"), Tecumseh began to organize a vast alliance to stem the flow. Tenskwatawa was the spiritual leader of the movement, preaching against white habits (especially drinking alcohol).

Tecumseh was the military and political leader, making epic journeys from the Great Lakes to the Gulf of Mexico to spread his message. He urged united opposition and rejected the right of

individual leaders to sell off land, which he felt belonged to all Native Americans. "We must be united," he told the Osage. "If you do not unite with us, they will first destroy us, and then you will fall easy prey to them. They have destroyed many nations of red men [tribespeople] because they were not united."

Traditional suspicions and rivalries stopped many tribes joining him, but many individuals ignored their leaders and left their tribes for Tecumseh's camp, called "Prophet's Town," on the Tippecanoe River. The camp soon aroused white fears, and an expedition led by William Henry Harrison, Tecumseh's great enemy, was sent against it. Harrison found the camp in September 1811,

while Tecumseh was away on a great trek south to recruit new tribes. Tenskwatawa launched an attack on the U.S. force, but he could not stop them burning the town and dispersing his men.

THE END OF A DREAM

Tecumseh was not yet beaten, and when the War of 1812 started, he sided with the British against the U.S. A Native-American alliance had not fully materialized, but with help from their "Great Father," King George III, Tecumseh hoped to expel the whites from his people's land. His dream was shattered, and his own life lost, at the Battle of the Thames in Ontario on October 5, 1813, which saw a complete U.S. victory.

ABOVE: Tecumseh is shown fighting in an attack on Fort Meigs in this hand-colored engraving.

SEE ALSO:
❖ Alcohol
❖ American Revolutionary War
❖ Indian Wars
❖ Osage
❖ Pontiac's War
❖ Settlers
❖ Shamanism
❖ Shawnee
❖ War of 1812

Tenochtitlán

Tenochtitlán was situated on the site of present-day Mexico City. The center of Tenochtitlán was established on an island off the western shore of Lake Texcoco, to which the Chichimec ancestors of the Aztecs had been banished. Tenochtitlán grew to become the capital of the Aztec civilization, and by the 16th century it was the largest city in the New World.

LAYOUT OF THE CITY

When it was founded about 1325, the city of Tenochtitlán (the name means "Place of the Cactus") was a small settlement of thatched houses. However, it developed into a vast capital of ceremonial sites, housing districts, and administrative buildings.

There were some 78 religious sites or shrines in Tenochtitlán, including temples and pyramids. The city was built on a geometrical pattern, and a system of canals criss-crossed between the islands. The inhabitants either traveled by canoe or walked across wooden bridges.

A series of giant causeways up to 16 feet (5 m) wide led into the center of the city. These causeways were raised by a system of draw-bridges that enabled vessels to pass through. The drawbridges also acted as a means of defense. Farther inside the city lay the giant plaza, 1,450 feet (440 m) wide, which was surrounded by ceremonial and reli-gious structures. Inside the plaza was the Teocalli—a site where ritual human sacrifices were made.

Tenochtitlán was divided into four districts subdivided into 80 "wards." The city's government promoted compulsory education, hygiene regulations, taxes, and military service for the male inhabitants. Tenochtitlán also had a defined social structure, with slaves at the lowest level. Most city-dwellers were either peasants or craftspeople.

DWELLINGS

The houses in Tenochtitlán were made from stone or clay bricks. Most had one story, but those belonging to wealthy citizens had two stories with flat-roof gardens. Houses were generally built around courtyards and were decorated with murals (colorful wall paintings), pottery, and flowers.

BELOW: This Spanish print depicting Tenochtitlán dates from 1576.

MEXICO.

MEXICO. REGIA ET CELEBRIS HISPANIE NOVAE CIVITAS.

Under Prince Nezahualcoyotl of Texcoco a dam was built to prevent floods. The dam also separated the salt water in the main lake from the fresh water of the city's lagoons. Ceramic pipes and troughs carried mountain spring water to fountains in the city. Tenochtitlán's public sanitation system was more advanced than that of any European city of the time.

Montezuma II was Tenochtitlán's ruler when the Aztecs first encountered Europeans. His palace covered some 6 acres (2.5 ha) and included civil, military, administrative, and residential areas. The palace also housed 3,000 servants, who maintained the king's quarters, gardens, game reserve, and treasury. Today the National Palace stands on its site.

CORTÉS AND THE SPANISH

The first European to reach Tenochtitlán was the Spanish conquistador Hernando Cortés in 1519. King Montezuma II allowed Cortés and his men to enter the city unhindered. Some historians argue that the king believed Cortés to be the Aztec god Quetzalcoatl and so allowed him easy access to the city.

Later, Montezuma II was killed during an uprising, and the Aztecs turned on the Spanish invaders. However, in the resulting siege Tenochtitlán's inhabitants were starved into submission. After plundering and torching the city, the Spanish drained the area. To assert their dominance and power, they then established a new capital on the site, which became Mexico City.

ABOVE: These Aztec stone-carved skulls, or "Tzompantli," were discovered at the site of El Templo Mayor in Mexico City.

SEE ALSO:

❖ Aztecs
❖ Chitchén Itzá
❖ Copán
❖ Cortés, Hernando
❖ Homes
❖ Palenque
❖ Pyramids

Thorpe, Jim

Part Sauk and part Fox, Jim Thorpe excelled at so many different sports that in 1950 almost 400 sports journalists voted him the best all-round athlete of the first half of the 20th century. His exploits on the football field and in track and field stand out the most, but he was also outstanding at baseball and more than competent at basketball, ice hockey, swimming, tennis, and boxing.

Thorpe was born in Keokuk Falls, Oklahoma, in 1888. At the well-known Carlisle Indian School in Pennsylvania from 1907 to 1912 he helped its football team to some famous victories over colleges such as Harvard. He made the all-American team in 1911 and 1912.

OLYMPIC GLORY

Thorpe's most famous feat came in 1912, when he won gold medals in both the pentathlon and decathlon at the Stockholm Olympics in Sweden, setting world records for total points scored in both events. But when it came to light that he had played semiprofessional baseball while taking a break from Carlisle, he was cruelly stripped of his medals—although they were restored by the Olympic Committee 30 years after his death.

Between 1913 and 1919 he played professional baseball for a number of teams, including the Boston Braves. After 1915 he also organized and played for the Bulldogs, a professional football team based in Canton, Ohio, and then for the New York Giants and Chicago Cardinals up to his retirement in 1929.

ABOVE: Jim Thorpe wins the 1,500-meter race, one of five events in the pentathlon, at the 1912 Olympics.

SEE ALSO:
❖ Games
❖ Movies
❖ Sauk and Fox

In the 1930s and early 1940s Thorpe appeared in movies and toured the country promoting Native-American interests. He then served in the U.S. Merchant Marine in World War II. In 1951 he was a technical advisor for a movie of his own life—starring the famous white actor Burt Lancaster as Thorpe.

Thorpe died in Lomita, California, in 1953. He was perhaps the first Native American to be widely accepted by the white people of his country as an all-American hero.

Tikal

LEFT: After the Maya deserted Tikal 1,000 or more years ago, the surrounding jungle quickly spread through the city, completely covering many of the buildings. Only the tops of the tallest pyramids protruded above the tree canopy.

Tikal is situated in the Petén region of western Guatemala. This major Mayan city-state lies in the middle of Central America's first national park, which covers some 220 square miles (570 sq. km). It is almost hidden by jungle, including Spanish cedar, a sacred Mayan tree. One of the largest Mayan sites ever excavated, Tikal was listed as a World Heritage monument by the United Nations in 1979.

A BUSTLING MAYAN CITY

Building in Tikal began about 800 B.C. and continued until about A.D. 900, when the Maya kingdoms declined, and the Maya abandoned the city. The city center covered 6 square miles (15 sq. km), and outlying residential areas 23 square miles (60 sq. km). At its peak, about A.D. 600, Tikal was a center of Mayan art, architecture, learning, and farming. At its height it may have had a population of 90,000.

Tikal contains some 4,000 structures, including palaces, temples, reservoirs, shrines, ballcourts, and plazas. The jungle, however, still covers many ruins, and looters have damaged many altars and carved stone columns.

At the center of Tikal is the Great Plaza, which is surrounded by temples built on terraced pyramids. The North Acropolis, begun about 2000 B.C., comprises several temples on a great platform and was the burial place of Tikal's kings for 3,000 years. Its Temple of the Jaguar, built about A.D. 870, rises 145 feet (43 m).

Originally such buildings were often plastered and decorated with bright red, orange, and blue paint. Since 1958 archaeologists have excavated over 100,000 artifacts, including jewelry, ornaments, ceremonial objects, and tools. These provide valuable information about the lives of the city's inhabitants.

Timucua

The Timucua people lived in eastern Florida. The Spanish conquistador, or conqueror, Ponce de León was the first European to make contact with them following his landfall in Florida in 1513.

At this time the Native-American population of this part of the Southeast was large, well structured, and hostile. Besides the Timucua, the warlike Calusa lived in the Everglades, the Apalachee in western Florida, and the Ais and Tequesta in between these regions.

Like these other tribes, the Timucua lived in palisaded, or fenced, villages ruled over by privileged chiefs who maintained a defined social hierarchy. The chiefs levied tribute on their domain and funded ceremonial complexes with some of the proceeds. This meant that warfare to force compliance and assert dominance was common—much as it was farther south in the Aztec empire.

ARMED RESISTANCE

In 1521 Ponce de León returned to Florida with missionaries, intent on forcing the local Native Americans to convert to Christianity. Spanish forays greatly provoked the Timucua, Calusa, and Apalachee, who resisted the Europeans fiercely. Ponce de León himself died of a wound inflicted by a poisoned dart fired from a Calusa blow-pipe.

The Spanish did not give up, however, and another conquistador, Hernando de Soto, took up the cause. He cemented a relationship

RIGHT: In this engraving the Timucua are shown firing burning arrows into the village of a rival Florida tribe.

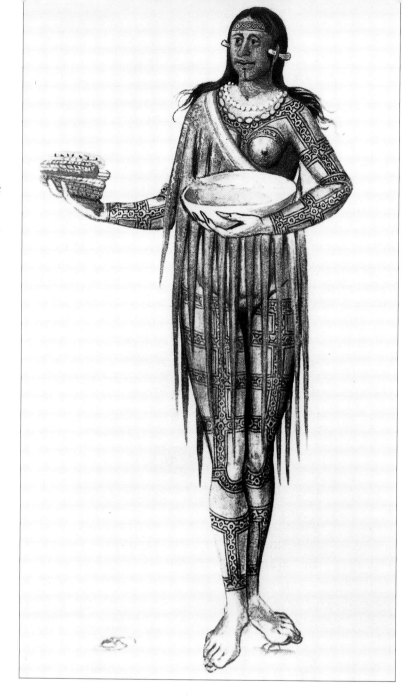

with the Timucua through a Spaniard who was living among them, having fled captivity from the Calusa, and had learned their language. This fortunate connection meant de Soto had local scouts and knowledge. His force cut a swathe through the tribes of the Southeast, trailing death and destruction to little real achievement.

In the decades that followed, the Spanish built settlements and forts—notably Fort Caroline and Fort Augustine—and Franciscan missionaries moved among the Timucua and other Florida tribes, making detailed records of their languages and customs.

VICTIMS OF THE SPANISH

The Timucua and other Florida tribes initially found themselves pawns in a battle between competing French Huguenot (Protestant), and Spanish Catholic missionaries. Spain prevailed, and their missions colonized Florida. About 1650 the Franciscans estimated the Timucua to number 10,000, with thousands more speaking their language in other related tribes, such as the Acuera.

Unfortunately for the Florida tribes their territories became the battleground for European powers competing for the spoils of a new continent. The Spanish controlled the region until 1763, when the British acquired Florida. The few remaining converted tribespeople fled with the Spanish. The more powerful Creek, allied to the British, moved into their territory. It is thought that the remaining Timucua and other victims of

ABOVE: Tattooing and other forms of body adornment were practiced by Timucua women as well as men. The Timucua woman depicted here is tattooed from head to ankle.

European settlement, such as the Yamasee, eventually merged into the Mikasuki and then the Seminole—so wiping out the Timucua as a distinct people.

SEE ALSO:
- ❖ Aztecs
- ❖ Body Adornment
- ❖ Bows and Arrows
- ❖ Extinction
- ❖ Missions
- ❖ Seminole
- ❖ Soto, Hernando de
- ❖ Southeast/ Florida

Tlingit

The Tlingit are a people of 14 tribes who live on the coast and islands of southern Alaska. Together with the Haida, Tsimshian, and Haisla, they make up the northern group of the Northwest Coast tribespeople. All share a complex, hierarchical fishing and gathering culture based on wealth and status.

Before they first made contact with Europeans in the 18th century, the Tlingit numbered an estimated 10,000 people. Because of the dense concentrations of people on the coast, fighting with neighboring tribes over land, particularly islands, was a constant feature of Tlingit life.

By the 1780s the Tlingit were trading with the Russians, swapping furs for guns and iron. They fought frequently with the Russians who settled in Alaska in the early 19th century. During this period a combination of European diseases and conflicts brought on by competition for trading goods severely reduced Tlingit numbers.

In 1971 the Tlingit and other tribes finally received some recompense, in the form of money and land, from the Alaska Native Claims Settlement Act. Today there are more than 14,000 Tlingit, many of whom work in the Alaskan logging and fishing industries.

A STRUCTURED SOCIETY

Tlingit society is based on lineages, clans, and two overall groups called moieties. The basic social unit is the lineage, with descent traced through the mother. Each lineage has its own chief, land, and ceremonies. Two or more lineages whose members can trace their descent from a common mythical ancestor make up a clan. Each clan has valued privileges, such as dances

BELOW: Engraved in 1802, this picture depicts a group of Tlingit warriors performing a war dance before attacking and destroying the Russian American Company's new settlement at Sitka.

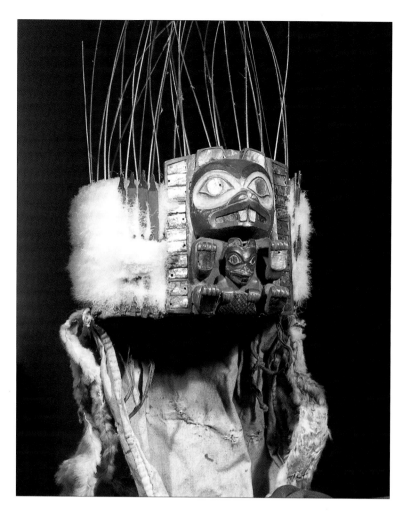

hunting, and carving were men's work, while women picked berries and looked after the home.

The Tlingit used wood, especially cedar, to make everything from canoes to bowls. The women blended cedar bark with wool from mountain goats to weave their renowned Chilkat blankets.

Potlatches—ceremonies at which gifts were given to reaffirm social status—were central to Tlingit life. The greater the gathering, the greater the status of the giver. They played a vital role at times of transition, such as the funeral of a clan chief. The new chief's family also gave a huge feast and gifts. By accepting his food and gifts, guests publicly recognized the new chief's status.

Like all Northwest Coast tribes, the Tlingit believed in respecting the animals they ate. Many of their religious practices were performed to placate animals' spirits so that in the future other animals would let themselves be caught. Each year the Tlingit thanked the first salmon they caught, then ritually returned the bones to the sea.

and masks, for ceremonies. Clan members belong to one of two moieties, Raven and Wolf—groups that cut across tribal boundaries. Marriage is always to someone outside one's own moiety.

SLAVES AND SALMON

Historically, Tlingit life was based around the activities of the most important families, who formed a class of nobles. Beneath the nobles were the common people and then slaves, who were captured or traded from other tribes.

The Tlingit economy was based mainly on fishing for salmon with harpoons, nets, and traps. Fishing,

ABOVE: Collected about 1900, this Tlingit headdress was for important ceremonies only. Made from ermine fur, swan feathers, whalebone, and sealion whiskers, it represents a large beaver holding a smaller beaver in its front legs.

SEE ALSO:
- Canoes
- Clan
- Dance
- Epidemics
- Fishing
- Fur Trade
- Haida
- Homes
- Land Rights
- Marriage
- Masks
- Medicine
- Northwest Coast
- Potlatch
- Rugs and Blankets
- Russia, Wars with
- Salmon
- Trade
- Tsimshian

Tobacco

Tobacco is native to North America and was unknown in Europe until the English explorer Sir Walter Raleigh introduced it as a medicinal plant at the end of the 15th century. Smoking dried tobacco leaves, and sniffing them in powder form as snuff, quickly became socially acceptable among the nobility in France, Portugal, Spain, and England. By the middle of the 16th century colonies such as Virginia generated a major part of their income from tobacco exports.

Native Americans rarely used tobacco socially. The variety they grew most, *Nicotiana rustica*, is a powerful stimulant. They used it mainly in ceremonies as an aid to establishing contact with the spirit world. Smoking tobacco "made the breath visible." Since breathing is the essence of life, tobacco smoke rising from Earth to the spiritual abode in the skies was seen by Native Americans as carrying their wishes and prayers heavenward.

CEREMONIAL CROP

Tobacco was cultivated in all the farming areas of North America. Some tribes who planted no other crops sometimes grew it ceremonially. For example, when the Crow split from the farming Hidatsa and became nomadic buffalo hunters, they retained a tradition of planting sacred tobacco in fields tended by only the most highly respected male elders. Even among farming tribes, caring for the sacred tobacco fields was seen as an honored occupation for men who had otherwise retired from active life as hunters and warriors.

The widespread use of tobacco by Native Americans in Pre-Contact North America is evident from finds

BELOW: The state of Virginia is well known for tobacco plantations, but the crop was grown by Native Americans throughout the U.S.

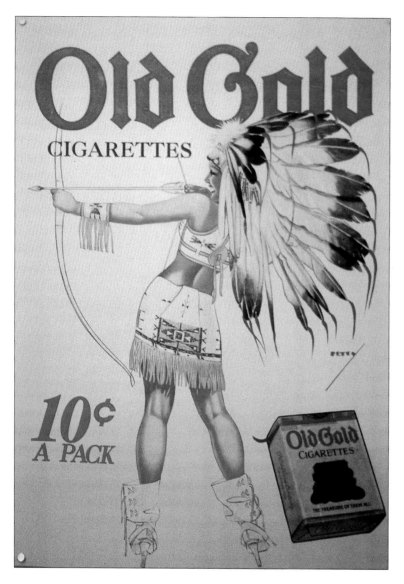

all, they smoked it in pipes called calumets. Commonly called peace pipes because they were used to seal bonds of friendship and non-aggression, they were also used to communicate directly with the spirit powers at important ceremonies. Calumets had elaborately decorated stems. Often they were covered with painted, quilled, or beaded hide and adorned with horsehair, cloth, beads, miniature flint arrow-heads or shells, and fans made from the wing feathers of eagles and other birds of prey.

Calumets probably originated in the East but soon became common among tribes along the Missouri and Mississippi rivers and on the Plains. Among the Blackfoot, for instance, calumet owners sealed pacts of friendship and led the way when the tribe moved camp, carrying the pipes to "clear the path."

It is said that any Native American entering a hostile camp with a pipe was welcomed and assured safe passage. Sharing pipes and offering guests tobacco are common customs still among Native Americans, and few ceremonies would be considered complete without their use.

at archaeological sites. The Anasazi, Mogollon, and Hohokam of the Southwest all planted tobacco, and the Adena and Hopewell of the Woodland and Southeast areas established a flourishing trade in tobacco and related products. Beautifully modeled figurine pipes depicting humans and animals have been found at many Hopewell sites.

Native Americans used tobacco in every way familiar today, such as rolling and smoking it as cigarettes and chewing it. Most famously of

ABOVE: Cigarette advertisements in the U.S. in the early 20th century often used stereotypical images of Native Americans to help sell the brand.

SEE ALSO:

- Adena and Hopewell
- Anasazi
- Blackfoot
- Crow
- Featherwork
- Hohokam
- Medicine
- Mogollon
- Plains
- Quillwork and Beadwork
- Ritual
- Southeast/Florida
- Southwest
- Trade
- Woodland

A–Z of Native-American Tribes

This A–Z provides a cultural summary of the major Native-American tribes. Where a tribe is the subject of an article in a particular volume of this set, the volume number and page reference are given. Also, alternative historical names for some tribes are shown inside parentheses.

A

ABNAKI (Abenaki)
LANGUAGE: Algonquian
AREA: Northeastern Woodland
HOUSING: Conical bark or mat houses in palisaded villages
NEIGHBORS: Passamaquoddy, Penobscot, Malecite, Micmac
LIFESTYLE: Hunting, fishing, farming
FOOD: Deer, corn, fish
CRAFTS: Quillwork, birchbark, skinwork

ACOMA 1:4
LANGUAGE: Keresan
AREA: Southwest
HOUSING: Multistory adobe
NEIGHBORS: Pueblo, Apache, Navajo, Zuni
LIFESTYLE: Settled farmers
FOOD: Corn, gathered foods, game
CRAFTS: Pottery, weaving

ALEUT (Unangan)
LANGUAGE: Eskimo-Aleut
AREA: Arctic (Aleutian Islands)
HOUSING: Semisubterranean sod- and driftwood-covered shelters
NEIGHBORS: Inuit, Tlingit
LIFESTYLE: Sea-mammal hunting, fishing
FOOD: Seals, shellfish, fish, whales, seabirds, plant foods
CRAFTS: Basketry, ivory carving, gut clothing

APACHE 1:36
LANGUAGE: Athapascan
AREA: Southwest
HOUSING: Brush-covered wickiups, some use of tepees
NEIGHBORS: Pueblo, Navajo, Comanche, Kiowa, Paiute
LIFESTYLE: Nomadic hunting-gathering, some farming
FOOD: Game, roots, berries, some buffalo, some corn
CRAFTS: Basketry, skinwork

ARAPAHO 1:41
LANGUAGE: Algonquian
AREA: Central Plains
HOUSING: Tepees
NEIGHBORS: Cheyenne, Shoshoni, Ute, Kiowa, Pawnee, Sioux
LIFESTYLE: Nomadic hunting
FOOD: Buffalo, deer, roots and berries
CRAFTS: Skin-, bead-, and featherwork

ARIKARA (Ree, Sahnish)
LANGUAGE: Caddoan
AREA: Upper Missouri (Northern Plains)
HOUSING: Earth lodges
NEIGHBORS: Mandan, Hidatsa, Sioux, Pawnee
LIFESTYLE: Some farming, hunting
FOOD: Corn, buffalo, deer, gathered roots and berries
CRAFTS: Skinwork, featherwork

ASSINIBOINE 1:49
LANGUAGE: Siouan
AREA: Northern Plains
HOUSING: Tepees
NEIGHBORS: Blackfoot, Crow, Sioux, Cree
LIFESTYLE: Nomadic hunting
FOOD: Buffalo, deer
CRAFTS: Quill-, bead-, and skinwork

ATHAPASCAN, Northern (Dine or Dene) 1:54
LANGUAGE: Athapascan
AREA: Western Subarctic
HOUSING: Bark-covered wigwams, bark lean-tos, log houses
NEIGHBORS: Inuit, Tlingit, Cree, Blackfoot
LIFESTYLE: Nomadic hunting, fishing, gathering
FOOD: Caribou, wild fowl, fish
CRAFTS: Quillwork, birchbark

B

BELLA BELLA (Heiltsuk)
LANGUAGE: Wakashan
AREA: Northwest Coast
HOUSING: Split cedar plank
NEIGHBORS: Bella Coola, Kwakiutl, Haida, Tsimshian
LIFESTYLE: Sea-mammal hunting, fishing
FOOD: Sea mammals, salmon, shellfish, roots and berries
CRAFTS: Woodcarving

BELLA COOLA (Tallion)
LANGUAGE: Salishan
AREA: Northwest Coast
HOUSING: Split cedar plank
NEIGHBORS: Bella Bella, Kwakiutl, Coast Salish
LIFESTYLE: Sea-mammal hunting, fishing
FOOD: Sea mammals, salmon, shellfish, roots and berries
CRAFTS: Woodcarving

BEOTHUK 2:5
LANGUAGE: Beothukan
AREA: Eastern Subarctic
HOUSING: Birchbark lodges
NEIGHBORS: Inuit, Naskapi, Micmac
LIFESTYLE: Hunting-gathering, fishing
FOOD: Deer, salmon, shellfish, gathered roots and berries
CRAFTS: Woodwork

BLACKFOOT (Siksika, Kainah, Piegan) 2:14
LANGUAGE: Algonquian
AREA: Northern Plains
HOUSING: Tepees
NEIGHBORS: Shoshoni, Crow, Sioux
LIFESTYLE: Nomadic hunting
FOOD: Buffalo, deer
CRAFTS: Quill-, bead-, and skinwork

C

CADDO Confederacy (Kadohadacho) 2:38
LANGUAGE: Caddoan
AREA: Southern Plains
HOUSING: Domed thatched houses
NEIGHBORS: Choctaw, Chickasaw, Wichita
LIFESTYLE: Farming and hunting
FOOD: Buffalo, deer, corn
CRAFTS: Woodcarving, basketry

CALUSA
LANGUAGE: Muskogean
AREA: Southern Florida
HOUSING: Palm-thatched shelters
NEIGHBORS: Timucua
LIFESTYLE: Fishing, hunting
FOOD: Fish, shellfish
CRAFTS: Woodcarving

CAYUSE
LANGUAGE: Penutian
AREA: Plateau
HOUSING: Rush mat-covered lodges, some use of tepees
NEIGHBORS: Shoshoni, Nez Percé, Flathead
LIFESTYLE: Hunting, fishing
FOOD: Deer, salmon, roots and berries
CRAFTS: Basketry, skinwork

CHEROKEE (Tsaragi)
LANGUAGE: Iroquoian
AREA: Southeast
HOUSING: Palisaded townships of log cabins
NEIGHBORS: Creek, Catawba
LIFESTYLE: Farming, some hunting
FOOD: Corn, beans, squash
CRAFTS: Woodcarving, basketry

CHEYENNE 2:56
LANGUAGE: Algonquian
AREA: Central Plains
HOUSING: Tepees
NEIGHBORS: Shoshoni, Arapaho, Sioux
LIFESTYLE: Nomadic hunting
FOOD: Buffalo, deer, gathered roots and berries
CRAFTS: Skin-, bead-, and featherwork

CHICKASAW
LANGUAGE: Muskogean
AREA: Southeast
HOUSING: Palisaded townships
NEIGHBORS: Choctaw, Caddo, Natchez, Creek
LIFESTYLE: Farming, some hunting
FOOD: Corn, beans, squash
CRAFTS: Basketry

CHINOOK (Tsi-Nuk) 3:4
LANGUAGE: Chinookan
AREA: Southern Northwest Coast
HOUSING: Semisubterranean split-plank houses
NEIGHBORS: Coast Salish, Klikitat
LIFESTYLE: Trading, fishing
FOOD: Salmon, game animals, gathered roots and berries
CRAFTS: Woodcarving

CHOCTAW (Chata)
LANGUAGE: Muskogean
AREA: Southeast
HOUSING: Palisaded townships
NEIGHBORS: Natchez, Chickasaw, Creek
LIFESTYLE: Farming, fishing, hunting

FOOD: Corn, beans, deer, birds, turtles, fish, nuts and berries
CRAFTS: Split-cane basketry

CHUGACH
LANGUAGE: Inuit
AREA: Western Arctic
HOUSING: Sod- and driftwood-covered lodges
NEIGHBORS: Tlingit, Northern Athapascan
LIFESTYLE: Sea-mammal hunting, hunting, fishing
FOOD: Sea mammals, shellfish, fish, caribou
CRAFTS: Ivory carving

CHUMASH 3:7
LANGUAGE: Chumashan (Hokan)
AREA: California
HOUSING: Thatched huts
NEIGHBORS: Mission Tribes, Yokut
LIFESTYLE: Sea-mammal hunting, fishing, gathering
FOOD: Sea mammals, shellfish, fish, plants and berries
CRAFTS: Shellwork, stonework, basketry

COAST SALISH 3:15
LANGUAGE: Salishan
AREA: Southern Northwest Coast
HOUSING: Split-plank houses
NEIGHBORS: Kwakiutl, Chinook
LIFESTYLE: Fishing, sea-mammal hunting
FOOD: Salmon, shellfish, seal, sea birds, roots and berries
CRAFTS: Woodcarving

COMANCHE 3:20
LANGUAGE: Uto-Aztecan
AREA: Southern Plains
HOUSING: Tepees
NEIGHBORS: Kiowa, Apache
LIFESTYLE: Nomadic hunting
FOOD: Buffalo, other game, gathered roots and berries
CRAFTS: Skinwork, beadwork

CREE (Knistenaux) 3:38
LANGUAGE: Algonquian
AREA: Subarctic
HOUSING: Bark-covered wigwams
NEIGHBORS: Athapascan, Inuit, Blackfoot, Ojibway
LIFESTYLE: Nomadic hunting-gathering, trapping, fishing
FOOD: Game animals, fish, gathered roots and berries
CRAFTS: Birchbark, quillwork, beadwork

CREEK (Muskogee)
LANGUAGE: Muskogean
AREA: Southeast
HOUSING: Palisaded townships
NEIGHBORS: Choctaw, Chickasaw, Cherokee, Timucua
LIFESTYLE: Farming
FOOD: Corn, beans, squash, game
CRAFTS: Cane basketry, silverwork

CROW (Apsaroke) 3:42
LANGUAGE: Siouan
AREA: Northern Plains
HOUSING: Tepees
NEIGHBORS: Blackfoot, Assiniboine, Sioux
LIFESTYLE: Nomadic hunting
FOOD: Buffalo, deer, gathered roots and berries
CRAFTS: Skin-, bead-, and featherwork

D

DELAWARE (Leni Lenape) 3:56
LANGUAGE: Algonquian
AREA: Eastern Woodland
HOUSING: Palisaded villages of bark lodges
NEIGHBORS: Iroquois, Woodland Algonquian
LIFESTYLE: Farming, hunting
FOOD: Corn, game, fish, gathered plants and berries
CRAFTS: Woodcarving, beadwork

F

FLATHEAD
LANGUAGE: Salishan
AREA: Plateau
HOUSING: Semisubterranean earth- or brush-covered pit houses
NEIGHBORS: Cayuse, Coeur D'Alene, Nez Percé
LIFESTYLE: Fishing, gathering, hunting
FOOD: Salmon, buffalo, deer, roots and berries
CRAFTS: Basketry, beadwork

G

GROS VENTRE (Atsina)
LANGUAGE: Algonquian
AREA: Northern Plains
HOUSING: Tepees
NEIGHBORS: Blackfoot, Crow, Assiniboine, Sioux
LIFESTYLE: Nomadic hunting
FOOD: Buffalo, deer, gathered roots and berries
CRAFTS: Beadwork, skinwork

H

HAIDA 4:43
LANGUAGE: Haida (distant link to Athapascan)
AREA: Northwest Coast
HOUSING: Split cedar plank
NEIGHBORS: Tlingit, Tsimshian
LIFESTYLE: Sea-mammal hunting, fishing
FOOD: Salmon, sea mammals, seabirds, some plant foods
CRAFTS: Woodcarving, basketry, argillite (a type of rock) carving

HIDATSA (Minnetaree)
LANGUAGE: Siouan
AREA: Northern Plains
HOUSING: Earth-lodge villages
NEIGHBORS: Mandan, Arikara, Sioux
LIFESTYLE: Farming, seasonal buffalo hunting
FOOD: Corn, beans, squash, vegetables, buffalo
CRAFTS: Skinwork, beadwork

HITCHITI
LANGUAGE: Muskogean
AREA: Southeast
HOUSING: Palisaded villages
NEIGHBORS: Creek, Cherokee
LIFESTYLE: Farming, some hunting
FOOD: Corn, beans, squash, game
CRAFTS: Basketry

HOPI (Moki) 4:50
LANGUAGE: Uto-Aztecan
AREA: Southwest
HOUSING: Multistory adobe
NEIGHBORS: Pueblo tribes, Navajo, Apache
LIFESTYLE: Farming
FOOD: Corn, beans, squash
CRAFTS: Weaving, basketry, woodwork

HUPA 4:61
LANGUAGE: Athapascan
AREA: Northern California
HOUSING: Cedar plank houses
NEIGHBORS: Yurok, Karok, Pomo
LIFESTYLE: Fishing, hunting, gathering
FOOD: Salmon, shellfish, acorns, game, roots and berries
CRAFTS: Shell engraving, fiber weaving, basketry, featherwork

HURON (Wendat, Wyandot, Tobacco) 4:62
LANGUAGE: Iroquoian
AREA: Northeast Woodland
HOUSING: Palisaded villages of bark-covered longhouses
NEIGHBORS: Ojibway, Potawatomi, Iroquois
LIFESTYLE: Farming, some hunting
FOOD: Corn, beans, squash, deer, gathered plant foods
CRAFTS: Quillwork, splint basketry, fiber weaving

I

INGALIK
LANGUAGE: Athapascan
AREA: Arctic
HOUSING: Brush, bark, and driftwood shelters
NEIGHBORS: Inuit, Tlingit
LIFESTYLE: Fishing, hunting
FOOD: Salmon, caribou, moose, waterfowl, roots and berries
CRAFTS: Skinwork, woodcarving, basketry

INUIT (Eskimo) 5:14
LANGUAGE: Inuit
AREA: Arctic
HOUSING: Snow houses (igloos), whalebone and driftwood shelters
NEIGHBORS: Northern Athapascan, Tlingit, Cree
LIFESTYLE: Nomadic hunting and fishing
FOOD: Sea mammals, whales, fish, caribou, some gathered foods
CRAFTS: Ivory carving

IOWA
LANGUAGE: Siouan
AREA: Eastern Plains
HOUSING: Dome-shaped earth lodges, tepees when hunting
NEIGHBORS: Sioux, Omaha, Oto
LIFESTYLE: Farming, seasonal buffalo hunting
FOOD: Corn, buffalo, deer, some gathered foods
CRAFTS: Skinwork, beadwork, some carved stonework

IROQUOIS Confederacy (Five Nations, Six Nations) 5:20
LANGUAGE: Iroquoian
AREA: Northeast Woodland
HOUSING: Stockaded villages of elm-bark-covered longhouses
NEIGHBORS: Huron, Ojibway, Northeast Woodland Algonquian
LIFESTYLE: Farming, some hunting and fishing
FOOD: Corn, beans, squash, maple syrup, nuts, roots, deer
CRAFTS: Skinwork, splint baskets, woodwork, shellwork

K

KANSA (Kaw)
LANGUAGE: Siouan
AREA: Eastern Plains
HOUSING: Dome-shaped earth lodges, tepees when hunting
NEIGHBORS: Pawnee, Oto, Osage
LIFESTYLE: Farming, seasonal buffalo hunting
FOOD: Corn, beans, buffalo, deer
CRAFTS: Skinwork, beadwork

KAROK
LANGUAGE: Karok (Hokan)
AREA: Northern California
HOUSING: Plank houses
NEIGHBORS: Yurok, Modoc, Hupa
LIFESTYLE: Fishing, hunting, gathering
FOOD: Salmon, other fish, acorns, gathered roots and berries
CRAFTS: Basketry, shellwork, featherwork

KICKAPOO (Kiwigapaw)
LANGUAGE: Algonquian
AREA: Great Lakes
HOUSING: Bark lodges in semi-permanent villages
NEIGHBORS: Sauk and Fox, Potawatomi, Winnebago
LIFESTYLE: Hunting, farming, gathering
FOOD: Game, fish, corn, wild rice
CRAFTS: Barkwork, beadwork, woven bags

KIOWA 5:37
LANGUAGE: Tanoan
AREA: Southern Plains
HOUSING: Tepees
NEIGHBORS: Comanche, Wichita, Kansa
LIFESTYLE: Nomadic buffalo hunting
FOOD: Buffalo, deer, gathered roots and berries
CRAFTS: Skin-, bead-, and featherwork

KIOWA-APACHE
LANGUAGE: Athapascan
AREA: Southern Plains
HOUSING: Tepees
NEIGHBORS: Kiowa, Comanche
LIFESTYLE: Nomadic buffalo hunting
FOOD: Buffalo, deer, gathered roots and berries
CRAFTS: Skin-, bead-, and featherwork

KLAMATH 5:42
LANGUAGE: Klamath
AREA: Northern California
HOUSING: Plank houses
NEIGHBORS: Takelma, Yurok, Karok
LIFESTYLE: Fishing, hunting
FOOD: Salmon, acorns, game, gathered roots and berries
CRAFTS: Basketry, some shell- and woodwork

KUTCHIN (Loucheux)
LANGUAGE: Athapascan
AREA: Western Subarctic
HOUSING: Skin wigwams, log houses
NEIGHBORS: Northern Athapascan, Inuit
LIFESTYLE: Hunting, fishing, gathering
FOOD: Caribou, moose, salmon, herring, roots and berries
CRAFTS: Skinwork, beadwork

KUTENAI
LANGUAGE: Kutenai
AREA: Plateau
HOUSING: Bark- and mat-covered
NEIGHBORS: Pend D'Oreille, Nez Percé
LIFESTYLE: Hunting, fishing, gathering
FOOD: Buffalo, deer, fish, gathered roots and berries
CRAFTS: Basketry, beadwork

KWAKIUTL 5:44
LANGUAGE: Wakashan
AREA: Northwest Coast
HOUSING: Split cedar plank
NEIGHBORS: Nootka, Coast Salish
LIFESTYLE: Sea-mammal hunting, fishing
FOOD: Salmon, sea mammals, shellfish, roots and berries
CRAFTS: Woodcarving, basketry

M
MAIDU
LANGUAGE: Maidu (Penutian)
AREA: Northern California
HOUSING: Earth-covered lodges
NEIGHBORS: Pomo, Miwok
LIFESTYLE: Fishing, gathering
FOOD: Fish, acorns, game, gathered roots and berries
CRAFTS: Basketry, featherwork

MANDAN (Mihwatoni)
LANGUAGE: Siouan
AREA: Northern Plains
HOUSING: Stockaded villages of domed earth lodges
NEIGHBORS: Hidatsa, Arikara, Sioux
LIFESTYLE: Farming, seasonal buffalo hunting
FOOD: Corn, beans, buffalo, deer, roots and berries
CRAFTS: Skinwork, beadwork

MENOMINEE
LANGUAGE: Algonquian
AREA: Great Lakes
HOUSING: Semipermanent bark lodge villages
NEIGHBORS: Winnebago, Sauk and Fox
LIFESTYLE: Hunting, farming, fishing
FOOD: Corn, wild rice, game, roots and berries
CRAFTS: Woodwork, woven bags, quillwork

MICMAC 6:29
LANGUAGE: Algonquian
AREA: Northeast Woodland
HOUSING: Bark and grass mat-covered wigwams
NEIGHBORS: Beothuk, Northeast Woodland Algonquian
LIFESTYLE: Hunting, fishing
FOOD: Fish, shellfish, moose, caribou, waterfowl, plant foods
CRAFTS: Quillwork, birchbark

MISSION INDIANS 6:33
LANGUAGE: Mainly Uto-Aztecan and Hokan
AREA: Southern California
HOUSING: Thatch shelters
NEIGHBORS: Chumash, Mohave, Yuma
LIFESTYLE: Fishing, gathering
FOOD: Fish, shellfish, acorns, rodents, roots and berries
CRAFTS: Basketry

MODOC 6:42
LANGUAGE: Penutian
AREA: Northern California
HOUSING: Plank houses
NEIGHBORS: Yurok, Karok, Hupa
LIFESTYLE: Fishing, hunting, gathering
FOOD: Fish, shellfish, deer, gathered plants and berries
CRAFTS: Beadwork, basketry

MOHAVE (Mojave)
LANGUAGE: Hokan
AREA: Southwest
HOUSING: Domed thatch houses, sometimes covered with sand
NEIGHBORS: Yuma, Apache, Pima, Papago
LIFESTYLE: Hunting, fishing, gathering
FOOD: Deer, fish, gathered roots and berries
CRAFTS: Beadwork, pottery dolls, bark weaving

MOHEGAN 6:50
LANGUAGE: Algonquian
AREA: Eastern Woodland
HOUSING: Villages of bark-covered houses
NEIGHBORS: Iroquois, Northeast Woodland Algonquian
LIFESTYLE: Farming, hunting
FOOD: Corn, beans, deer, gathered roots and berries
CRAFTS: Basketry

MONTAGNAIS
LANGUAGE: Algonquian
AREA: Eastern Subarctic
HOUSING: Birchbark-covered wigwams
NEIGHBORS: Naskapi, Cree
LIFESTYLE: Hunting
FOOD: Caribou, moose, gathered plant foods, some fish
CRAFTS: Skinwork, birchbark

N
NASKAPI 7:4
LANGUAGE: Algonquian
AREA: Eastern Subarctic
HOUSING: Birchbark-covered wigwams
NEIGHBORS: Montagnais, Cree, Inuit
LIFESTYLE: Hunting, fishing, some gathering
FOOD: Caribou, moose, waterfowl, some gathered plant foods
CRAFTS: Caribou skinwork, birchbark

NATCHEZ (Avoyel) 7:6
LANGUAGE: Natchez
AREA: Southeast
HOUSING: Palisaded townships, thatched cabins on earth mounds
NEIGHBORS: Caddo, Chickasaw, Choctaw
LIFESTYLE: Farming, some hunting
FOOD: Corn, sunflowers, melons, deer, some gathered foods
CRAFTS: Basketry, weaving

NAVAJO (Dine or Dene) 7:9
LANGUAGE: Athapascan
AREA: Southwest
HOUSING: Hogans
NEIGHBORS: Apache, Pueblo
LIFESTYLE: Seminomadic hunting and gathering, herding, farming

FOOD: Small game, gathered roots and berries, corn
CRAFTS: Weaving, silverwork

NEZ PERCÉ (Chute-Pa-Lu) 7:13

LANGUAGE: Penutian
AREA: Plateau
HOUSING: Cattail mat multifamily houses, some tepees
NEIGHBORS: Flathead, Cayuse, Shoshoni
LIFESTYLE: Fishing, hunting, gathering
FOOD: Salmon, buffalo, deer, gathered roots and berries
CRAFTS: Basketry, woven bags, skinwork, beadwork

NOOTKA (Nuu-Chah-Nulth) 7:19

LANGUAGE: Wakashan
AREA: Northwest Coast
HOUSING: Split cedar plank
NEIGHBORS: Coast Salish, Kwakiutl
LIFESTYLE: Sea-mammal hunting, whaling, fishing
FOOD: Seals, whales, salmon, shellfish, roots and berries
CRAFTS: Woodcarving, basketry, some shellwork

O

OJIBWAY (CHIPPEWA; also Saulteaux, Flambeaux, Pillagers, Anishinabe) 7:24

LANGUAGE: Algonquian
AREA: Great Lakes
HOUSING: Large villages of bark-covered wigwams
NEIGHBORS: Cree, Ottawa, Iroquois
LIFESTYLE: Farming, hunting, fishing, gathering
FOOD: Caribou, moose, fish, wild rice, maple syrup, fruits
CRAFTS: Basketry, birchbark, wood-carving, rush weaving

OMAHA

LANGUAGE: Siouan
AREA: Eastern Plains
HOUSING: Earth lodge villages, tepees when hunting
NEIGHBORS: Pawnee, Sioux, Iowa, Oto
LIFESTYLE: Farming, seasonal buffalo hunting
FOOD: Corn, buffalo, deer, gathered plant foods
CRAFTS: Skinwork, beadwork, ribbon appliqué

OSAGE 7:32

LANGUAGE: Siouan
AREA: Eastern Plains
HOUSING: Earth lodge villages, tepees when hunting
NEIGHBORS: Pawnee, Kiowa, Caddo
LIFESTYLE: Farming, seasonal buffalo hunting
FOOD: Corn, buffalo, deer, gathered plant foods
CRAFTS: Skinwork, beadwork, ribbon appliqué

OTO

LANGUAGE: Siouan
AREA: Eastern Plains
HOUSING: Earth lodge villages, tepees when hunting
NEIGHBORS: Pawnee, Osage, Sioux
LIFESTYLE: Farming, seasonal buffalo hunting
FOOD: Corn, buffalo, deer, gathered plant foods
CRAFTS: Skinwork, beadwork

OTTAWA

LANGUAGE: Algonquian
AREA: Great Lakes
HOUSING: Villages of bark-covered wigwams
NEIGHBORS: Ojibway, Cree, Iroquois
LIFESTYLE: Farming, fishing, hunting, gathering
FOOD: Wild rice, fish, game, gathered roots and berries
CRAFTS: Quillwork, birchbark

P

PAIUTE (Chemehuevi) 7:36

LANGUAGE: Uto-Aztecan
AREA: Great Basin
HOUSING: Brush-covered wickiups, some use of tepees
NEIGHBORS: Ute, Shoshoni
LIFESTYLE: Nomadic hunting and gathering
FOOD: Small game, birds, roots and berries, insects, reptiles
CRAFTS: Basketry, rabbitskin blankets

PAPAGO (Tohono-O-Otam) 7:45

LANGUAGE: Uto-Aztecan
AREA: Southwest
HOUSING: Thatched wickiups
NEIGHBORS: Pima, Apache, Mohave
LIFESTYLE: Farming, hunting, gathering, fishing
FOOD: Corn, beans, squash, deer, roots and berries, some fish
CRAFTS: Basketry

PAWNEE (Skidi, Kitkehaxki, Pitahaurata, Chaui) 7:49

LANGUAGE: Caddoan
AREA: Eastern Plains
HOUSING: Earth lodge villages
NEIGHBORS: Sioux, Arapaho, Kiowa, Osage
LIFESTYLE: Farming, seasonal buffalo hunting
FOOD: Corn, beans, squash, buffalo, deer, roots and berries
CRAFTS: Skinwork, beadwork

PEQUOT

LANGUAGE: Algonquian
AREA: Eastern Woodland
HOUSING: Stockaded towns of bark-covered lodges
NEIGHBORS: Northeast Woodland Algonquian
LIFESTYLE: Farming, some hunting and gathering
FOOD: Corn, beans, squash, deer, gathered roots and berries
CRAFTS: Quillwork, beadwork

PIMA (Ah-Kee-Mult-O-O-Tam) 7:45

LANGUAGE: Uto-Aztecan
AREA: Southwest
HOUSING: Thatched wickiups
NEIGHBORS: Papago, Apache, Mohave
LIFESTYLE: Farming, hunting, gathering, fishing
FOOD: Corn, beans, squash, deer, roots, berries, mesquite, fish
CRAFTS: Basketry

POMO 7:60

LANGUAGE: Pomo (Hokan)
AREA: Central California
HOUSING: Tule-covered lodges
NEIGHBORS: Hupa, Wintun, Miwok
LIFESTYLE: Hunting, fishing, gathering
FOOD: Game, fish, acorns, gathered roots and berries
CRAFTS: Basketry, featherwork

PONCA

LANGUAGE: Siouan
AREA: Eastern Plains
HOUSING: Villages of earth lodges, tepees when hunting
NEIGHBORS: Sioux, Pawnee, Omaha
LIFESTYLE: Farming, seasonal buffalo hunting
FOOD: Corn, vegetables, buffalo, deer, gathered roots and berries
CRAFTS: Skinwork, beadwork

POTAWATOMI
LANGUAGE: Algonquian
AREA: Northeast Woodland
HOUSING: Bark-covered lodges
NEIGHBORS: Sauk and Fox,
   Kickapoo, Iroquois
LIFESTYLE: Farming, fishing,
   some hunting and gathering
FOOD: Corn, fish, deer, wild plants
   and roots
CRAFTS: Beadwork, ribbon appliqué,
   birchbark

POWHATAN Confederacy
LANGUAGE: Algonquian
AREA: Eastern Woodland
HOUSING: Palisaded villages of
   thatch- or bark-covered lodges
NEIGHBORS: Northeast Woodland
   Algonquian
LIFESTYLE: Farming, some hunting
   and gathering
FOOD: Corn, beans, squash, deer,
   gathered plant foods
CRAFTS: Beadwork

PUEBLO 8:17
LANGUAGE: Tanoan and Keresan
AREA: Southwest
HOUSING: Multistory adobe
NEIGHBORS: Apache, Navajo
LIFESTYLE: Farming, some hunting
FOOD: Corn, beans, squash, deer,
   gathered roots and berries
CRAFTS: Pottery, silverwork, weaving

S

SALISH 8:57
LANGUAGE: Salishan
AREA: Plateau
HOUSING: Semisubterranean brush-
   or earth-covered lodges
NEIGHBORS: Blackfoot, Nez Percé,
   Cayuse
LIFESTYLE: Fishing, hunting, trapping,
   and gathering
FOOD: Salmon, river fish, deer, wild
   roots and berries
CRAFTS: Basketry

SAUK and FOX
(Sac, Mesquakie) 8:63
LANGUAGE: Algonquian
AREA: Great Lakes
HOUSING: Bark-covered lodges,
   tepees when hunting
NEIGHBORS: Kickapoo, Sioux
LIFESTYLE: Farming, gathering,
   trapping, seasonal hunting
FOOD: Corn, beans, squash, wild rice,
   buffalo, roots and berries

CRAFTS: Quillwork, woven bags,
   ribbon appliqué

SEMINOLE 9:7
LANGUAGE: Muskogean
AREA: Florida
HOUSING: Palm-thatched chickees
   raised on stilts
NEIGHBORS: Miccosukee
LIFESTYLE: Fishing, hunting,
   farming
FOOD: Corn, beans, shellfish, fish,
   roots
CRAFTS: Ribbon patchwork

SHAWNEE 9:22
LANGUAGE: Algonquian
AREA: Southeast
HOUSING: Palisaded townships
NEIGHBORS: Kickapoo, Creek
LIFESTYLE: Farming, some hunting
FOOD: Corn, deer, gathered roots
   and berries
CRAFTS: Beadwork, some pottery

SHOSHONI (Tsosoni)
LANGUAGE: Uto-Aztecan
AREA: Western Plains
HOUSING: Brush-covered wickiups,
   tepees
NEIGHBORS: Blackfoot, Cheyenne,
   Arapaho, Ute, Paiute
LIFESTYLE: Nomadic hunting and
   gathering
FOOD: Buffalo in East, wild plant
   foods in West
CRAFTS: Skinwork, beadwork

SIOUX
(Dakota, Lakota, Nakota) 9:27
LANGUAGE: Siouan
AREA: Northern and Eastern Plains
HOUSING: Tepees
NEIGHBORS: Blackfoot, Crow,
   Cheyenne, Arapaho, Winnebago
LIFESTYLE: Nomadic hunting and
   gathering
FOOD: Buffalo, deer, wild plants
CRAFTS: Skinwork, beadwork

T

TAOS (Tua) 9:51
LANGUAGE: Tanoan
AREA: Southwest
HOUSING: Multistory adobe
NEIGHBORS: Pueblo tribes, Apache,
   Navajo
LIFESTYLE: Farming
FOOD: Corn, beans, squash,
   some game, gathered foods
CRAFTS: Pottery, some basketry

TIMUCUA (Utina) 9:59
LANGUAGE: Timucuan (related to
   Muskogean)
AREA: Florida
HOUSING: Villages of palm-
   thatched houses
NEIGHBORS: Calusa, Apalachee
LIFESTYLE: Farming, hunting,
   fishing
FOOD: Corn, beans, fish, birds,
   alligators, plant foods
CRAFTS: Pottery

TLINGIT 9:61
LANGUAGE: Tlingit (related to
   Athapascan)
AREA: Northern Northwest Coast
HOUSING: Split cedar plank
NEIGHBORS: Tsimshian, Chugach,
   Inuit, Northern Athapascan
LIFESTYLE: Trading, sea-mammal
   hunting, fishing
FOOD: Salmon, other fish, sea
   mammals, shellfish
CRAFTS: Woodcarving, basketry,
   weaving

TSIMSHIAN 10:23
LANGUAGE: Chimmesyan (related to
   Penutian)
AREA: Northwest Coast
HOUSING: Split cedar plank
NEIGHBORS: Tlingit, Haida,
   Bella Bella
LIFESTYLE: Trading, sea-mammal
   hunting, fishing
FOOD: Salmon, other fish, sea
   mammals, shellfish
CRAFTS: Woodcarving, basketry

U

UTE (Nunt'z)
LANGUAGE: Uto-Aztecan
AREA: Great Basin
HOUSING: Brush-covered wickiups
NEIGHBORS: Paiute, Shoshoni,
   Navajo
LIFESTYLE: Nomadic gathering
FOOD: Small game, reptiles,
   insects, plants, roots and berries
CRAFTS: Basketry, beadwork

W

WICHITA
LANGUAGE: Caddoan
AREA: Southern Plains
HOUSING: Domed thatched houses
NEIGHBORS: Kiowa, Comanche,
   Caddo Confederacy
LIFESTYLE: Farming, hunting

FOOD: Corn, buffalo, deer, gathered roots and berries
CRAFTS: Skinwork, beadwork

WINNEBAGO
LANGUAGE: Siouan
AREA: Great Lakes
HOUSING: Earth- or bark-covered houses, tepees when hunting
NEIGHBORS: Sauk and Fox, Potawatomi
LIFESTYLE: Farming, seasonal hunting
FOOD: Corn, buffalo, deer, wild rice, fish, roots and berries
CRAFTS: Pottery, skin-, quill- and beadwork

WINTUN
LANGUAGE: Wintun (Penutian)
AREA: Central California
HOUSING: Mat-covered lodges
NEIGHBORS: Pomo, Maidu
LIFESTYLE: Hunting, fishing, gathering

FOOD: Salmon, deer, acorns, gathered roots and berries
CRAFTS: Basketry, featherwork, some woodwork

Y

YAQUI
LANGUAGE: Uto-Aztecan
AREA: Southwest
HOUSING: Villages of thatched lodges
NEIGHBORS: Pima, Papago, Apache
LIFESTYLE: Farming, hunting, gathering
FOOD: Corn, small game, gathered roots and berries
CRAFTS: Skinwork, some woodcarving

YUMA (Quechan)
LANGUAGE: Hokan
AREA: Southwest
HOUSING: Thatched lodges
NEIGHBORS: Mohave, Papago, Pima, Apache
LIFESTYLE: Farming, hunting, gathering

FOOD: Corn, melons, deer, gathered roots and berries
CRAFTS: Beadwork, pottery dolls

YUROK (Weitspekan)
LANGUAGE: Yurok
AREA: Northern California
HOUSING: Driftwood or plank
NEIGHBORS: Klamath, Karok, Modoc
LIFESTYLE: Hunting, fishing, gathering
FOOD: Deer, fish, roots and berries
CRAFTS: Shellwork, basketry

Z

ZUNI (A'shiwi) 10:62
LANGUAGE: Zunian
AREA: Southwest
HOUSING: Multistory adobe
NEIGHBORS: Pueblo, Apache, Navajo
LIFESTYLE: Farming, some hunting
FOOD: Corn, beans, squash, small game, some gathered plants
CRAFTS: Pottery, weaving, woodcarving, silverwork

FURTHER READING

Calloway, C. G. *New Worlds for All: Indians, Europeans, and the Remaking of Early America*. Baltimore, MD: Johns Hopkins University Press, 1997.

Edmonds, S. and P. Kernaghan. *Native Peoples of North America: Diversity and Development*. New York: Cambridge University Press, 1994.

Hirschfelder, A., ed. *Nature Heritage: Personal Accounts by American Indians, 1790 to the Present*. New York: Macmillan, General Reference, 1995.

Hoxie, F. E. *Encyclopedia of North American Indians*. Boston, MA: Houghton Mifflin Co., 1996.

Hyslop, S. G. and H. Woodhead, eds. *Chroniclers of Indian Life*. Alexandria, VA: Time Life, 1996.

Johnson, M. G. and R. Hook. *The Native Tribes of North America: A Concise Encyclopedia*. New York: Macmillan, 1994.

Josephy, A. M. *500 Nations: An Illustrated History of North American Indians*. New York: Knopf, 1998.

Keller, R. H. and M. F. Turek. *American Indians and National Parks*. Tuscon, AZ: University of Arizona Press, 1998.

Long, A. and M. Boldt. *Governments in Conflict: Provinces and Indian Nations in Canada*. Toronto, Ontario: University of Toronto Press, 1998.

Maynard, J., ed. *Through Indian Eyes: The Untold Story of Native American Peoples*. Pleasantville, NY: Readers Digest, 1996.

Meltzer, D. J. *Search for the First Americans*. Washington, DC: Smithsonian Books, 1995.

Miller, L., ed. *From the Heart: Voices of the American Indian*. New York: Knopf, 1995.

Nichols, R. L. *Indians in the United States and Canada: A Comparative History*. Lincoln, NE: University of Nebraska Press, 1998.

Pritzker, B. *Native Americans: An Encyclopedia of History, Culture, and Peoples*. Santa Barbara, CA: ABC-Clio, 1998.

Sperber, C. and A. J. Joffe. *The First Immigrants from Asia: A Population History of the North American Indians*. New York: Plenum Publishing Corporation, 1992.

Steele, I. K. *Warpaths: Invasions of North America*. New York: Oxford University Press, 1994.

Thornton, R., ed. *Studying Native America: Problems and Prospects*. Madison, WI: University of Wisconsin Press, 1999.

Trigger, B. G. and W. E. Washburn, eds. *The Cambridge History of the Native Peoples of the Americas: North America*. New York: Cambridge University Press, 1996.

Turner, G. *Indians of North America*. New York: Sterling Publications, 1992.

Waldrum, C. and M. Braun. *Atlas of the North American Indian*. New York: Facts on File, 1995.

Warhus, M. *Another America: Native American Maps and the History of Our Land*. New York: St. Martin's Press, 1997.

SET INDEX

Volume numbers and page numbers for main entries are shown in **bold**. Page numbers of illustrations or picture captions are shown in *italic*. Additional references can be found in the SEE ALSOS at the ends of the main entries.

ACKNOWLEDGMENTS

Picture Credits

B. & C. Alexander: 38; Ancient Art & Architecture: 14; Brown Part-works: National Archives 48; Corbis: 27, Bettmann 42, 45, Richard A. Cooke 15; Getty Images: 58; Hulton-Getty Picture Library: 12, 20, 57, 59, 61; Mary Evans Picture Library 32; Peter Newark Historical Pictures: 4, 5, 6, 7, 11, 13, 18, 22, 23, 29, 31, 33, 37, 43, 51, 55; Northwind Picture Archive: 16, 19, 34, 36, 41, 44, 53, 54, 63; Mick Sharpe: 52; Sylvia Bancroft Hunt Pictures: 8–9, 10, 21, 26, 50, 60, 64; Werner Forman Archive: 24, 25, 28, 35, 39, 46, 47, 49, 56, 62.

Text Contributors

Norman Bancroft Hunt, Steven L. Grafe, Ray Granger, Jen Green, Charlotte Greig, Casey Horton, Chris Marshall, Nigel Ritchie, Antony Shaw, Stephen Small, Donald Sommerville, Chris Westhorp.